REACH!

Dream | Stretch | Achieve | Influence

Stacey Alcorn with
Christi Guthrie & Ann Marie DuRoss

authorHOUSE®

AuthorHouse™
1663 Liberty Drive
Bloomington, IN 47403
www.authorhouse.com
Phone: 1-800-839-8640

Published by AuthorHouse 10/24/2013

ISBN: 978-1-4918-1665-3 (sc)
ISBN: 978-1-4918-1795-7 (hc)
ISBN: 978-1-4918-1666-0 (e)

Library of Congress Control Number: 2013917999

This book is dedicated to Adriana, Drew, Lily, Mack, Michael, and Oshyn. May you one day realize that your REACH! is far beyond your fingertips and to Joey Middlemiss who proved in his six short years that for some, REACH! extends an eternity.

Table of Contents

Foreword by Christi Guthrie
What's Stopping You?

Whether you're a man or woman, we were all raised on the same stories of princesses and princes trotting off into the sunset to live "Happily Ever After." These stories often program our collective subconscious to think that women can sit and wait for her man to find her and care for her needs without mention of his own and then everything in life will be all sunshine and rainbows. Today I look at these fairy tales in a different light; I see those princesses and princes *REACH!ing* for what each of them wants, chasing down evil and vaulting every obstacle until they obtain whatever they are after. Heck, even Ariel didn't let having no legs stop her quest for the love she was after. I challenge you all to find the REACH! that each fabled character displays when reading these tales to your children. Hidden in the fabric of each story is a timeless message for young and old: Good things come to those who REACH!. Stacey, Ann Marie, and I don't consider ourselves princesses in waiting but rather princesses with *prowess*, hunting down our latest desires. We have learned to reprogram our minds to see another story within our childhood tales—and we implore you do to the same.

Every day we have a choice to wait until something/someone knocks on our door or to REACH! for our own happiness. You can play the victim or the valiant warrior. Nothing is stopping you! Don't fall victim to your own apathy or fear. REACH! for knowledge. REACH! to broaden your sphere of influence. REACH! for better choices financially, physically, and mentally. There are REACH! choices all around us, from the education we pursue to the people we associate with, and right down to the books we read or the food we eat. The REACH! movement is about everyday living, climbing each mountain, making better choices, and chasing down dreams. It is about becoming an *awesomer you*! REACH! nourishes the mind, body, and soul. It strengthens confidence and know-how while diminishing fears and ignorance.

We celebrate you for REACH!ing for *REACH!*. Cheers to opening a door that will change your perspective on living, being, and existing. We are all a part of a whole, no more than six degrees removed from everyone else living today. If we all began practicing the art of REACH! as spelled out in this book, life as a whole would be a better, happier experience for us all and filled with countless more "Happily Ever Afters." Here's to yours; enjoy!

– Christi Guthrie, Entrepreneur, Stylist,
Huffington Post Blogger, and REACH!er Extraordinaire

"Twenty years from now you will be more disappointed by the things you didn't do than by the ones you did. So throw off the bowlines. Sail away from the safe harbor. Catch the trade winds in your sails. Explore. Dream. Discover...."
— *Mark Twain*

"And REACH!!"
— *Stacey Alcorn, Ann Marie DuRoss, and Christi Guthrie*

Visit www.theREACHmovement.com for free downloadable REACH! tools.

Stacey   **Ann Marie**   **Christi**

Chapter 1

Reach

Verb

To stretch out an arm in a specified direction in order to touch or grasp something: "He reached over and turned off his bedside light."

Noun

An act of reaching out with one's arm: "She made a reach for him."

Synonyms

verb.	attain - arrive - extend - gain - come - get - achieve

noun.	scope - range - stretch - extent

Chapter 2

REACH!

"Every great dream begins with a dreamer. Always remember, you have within you the strength, the patience, and the passion to reach for the stars to change the world." – Harriet Tubman

Today is a rainy, muggy, dreary Monday in June. It's just an ordinary day, except for one thing. Today is one of those days I decided to REACH!. What is REACH! as opposed to reach? REACH! with an exclamation point portrays emotion. It is me yelling to you. It's tiny, five foot tall me, raised to my tippy toes on the sidelines of your life screaming from the top of my lungs to you, "REACH! Damn it! REACH!.."

So who, exactly, am I? Let's back up a bit.

As I write this in 2013, I am co-owner of one of the largest real estate organizations in Massachusetts with fourteen offices throughout the state. I also own a fairly large and thriving law practice, a coaching and consulting firm, and a fashion business. I have written a few books now, and I blog weekly for *The Huffington Post* and other outlets. I am forty years old, engaged to be married to my amazing fiancé, Jay, and mom to my three-year-old daughter, Oshyn.

I don't share my accomplishments to boast, because they are really not much to boast about. I haven't yet accomplished all of my dreams, but I am working on them daily and have made great headway. And today seemed as good a day as any to share my thoughts about success in the sincere hope that they will inspire you to attain your own version of success. I admit that this book is a bit self-serving, too; it serves as a reminder to me that REACH! got me to where I am today—and will quite likely help take me where I want to go next. So off we go together…

I read Sheryl Sandberg's book, *Lean In*. If there is such a thing as a Biggest Fan, then I am hers. I agree with Sheryl that we need more women CEOs. I laud her for telling the world that we need more great men to pick up the slack at home. Bravo to her for making it ok to really love your high-level, executive job so much that you are willing to head off to work when your three-year-old is clinging to your leg yelling, "Mom, please don't go!" like mine does.

If you haven't read *Lean In*, you should. But read this book first—not because one's better than the other, but because mine starts earlier in your process of attainment. "Leaning In" is great if you are already sitting on the doorstep of the opportunity you are seeking. I would venture to guess, however, that most people are not even close to where they want to be. In fact, they are so far away that if they simply "Lean In" they will fall to their death in a great, deep, dark crevasse of the unknown.

So what do you do if you are simply not that close to your ideal opportunity? If you're too far from what you want to "Lean In," now is the time to REACH! out.

This book is about magic. It is about creating something out of nothing. It is about bravely closing your eyes, pushing through your fear, and reaching for something that is not yet within your grasp. Once armed with the lessons and stories in this book, you will have the essential skills needed to achieve all of your dreams. For the first time ever, the job you want, the spouse you seek, the house, the car, the education, and the accomplishments you yearn for are all within REACH!. If this sounds unlikely or even impossible, keep reading, as I share back-to-back stories of people like you who thought that their greatest aspirations were pipe dreams too. Then something amazing happened in each of the lives I showcase in this book. They learned a skill never taught in school, rarely dissected in books, and seldom talked about amongst peers. They learned how to REACH!.

If Sandberg's *Lean In* is considered a Master's degree toward attaining your life dreams, then consider this book your Bachelor's.

REACH! has two meanings that I will share interchangeably throughout this book. First, REACH! is the act of pursuing something even if you can't see it. It is the power within you to bridge the gap between where you are right this second and where you want to be. REACH! is the single best predictor of your future.

Second, REACH! represents the power of multiples. It is the people who you influence. It is your family, friends, customers, community, and the rest of your entire network. Leveraged wisely, this type of REACH! will accelerate your journey to the tomorrow that you have so far only envisioned. On the voyage to your greatest dreams, would you prefer to take a horse and buggy or a Learjet? You have a Learjet parked right out back and that is your network. In this book, I will teach you how to REACH! out to your network and hop aboard that jet.

Growing up in the suburbs of Boston, my family was considered middle-class. My dad was a self-employed auto-mechanic (and still is). My mom stayed home with me and my younger sister and brother. We weren't rich, but we were comfortable. Most of what I learned about business came from my dad, the sole income earner in our family. He taught me many of the REACH! principles I share in this book, first and foremost that hard work and treating your customers fairly and honestly creates incredible REACH!. I have applied these lessons in every business I have owned. They are simple philosophies, but they are effective. I know they work because I have used them to get where I am today.

I graduated from high school in 1990. I was rejected from literally every college I applied to. I had no idea that my grades were so poor. I will readily admit that I am quite social and when offered the choice between studying in high school and going on joyrides with my friends to shop, party, or just relax on the beach, I always chose the latter. I never thought about the consequences, but who really does at seventeen?

Upon graduation, I had $100 saved up (all from my graduation party) and a job: copy machine girl at a local mortgage company. I was making some money, and nobody in my family was overly concerned that I wasn't heading to college. In fact, they seemed a bit relieved seeing as though they wouldn't have to pay for it. We were not the type of family that set college as the expectation, which meant there was definitely no money put aside for that purpose.

But the stark reality of lacking direction hit me hard that summer after graduation. My friends were all going off to college and I felt left behind with no plans at all other than to make copies of mortgage packages—forever. It bothered me. Nobody pushed me into wanting more for myself, but I did. I had big dreams. I had visions of being an entrepreneur someday. I knew I was meant for greatness.

So that summer, I signed up for the one school that I knew would take me: a local community college. I asked my mortgage company to keep me on full time so I could pay for school, even if it meant working some really flexible hours, and they agreed. The great thing about being a copy girl is that copies could get made just as easily during off-business hours. I had applied to school late so my first semester was not going to qualify for financial aid. I was going to have to spend every dime of my paycheck on my education—and that's exactly what I did.

I completed my first semester at community college with nearly perfect grades, and nearly perfect attendance. It was the very first time in my life that I REACH!ed for something and grabbed it. The thrill was exhilarating and I wanted more of it! I didn't *Lean In* and take something that was presented to me. No, I invented something I wanted, a college education, and I REACH!ed for it. That's the funny thing about REACH!. When you do it, you stretch your muscles long and you just know there's more within you.

I finished my second semester at the community college just as strong as the first. Wow! Now I was onto something. I knew for certain that the first semester wasn't a fluke. I could actually carry a full-time job and a full workload at school. If I could do that, I knew I could do anything.

I still had two semesters left to attain my Associate's degree.

This was going to be big news in my family, something that none of them had ever expected. A college graduate sleeping in *their* home! The more I thought about all I'd REACH!ed for and pulled closer to me, the more confident I became. I loved the thrill of the REACH!! I wanted to go after bigger and better things in my life.

As Graduation Day approached, my family was busy planning my grand party. But I was already focusing on my next REACH!. I recalled that the most accomplished student in my high school class had been accepted to Bentley College (now Bentley University), the best business school in New England. Bentley was well renowned for producing affluent business leaders from around the world and just happened to be a forty-minute drive from my house. Could I afford it? I had already accumulated a small amount of student loan debt, but it wasn't much since every penny I earned at my job went toward paying the tuition I had racked up so far. Was it possible that someone like me, who got rejected from her own state's public university two years earlier, could get into Bentley? What would happen if I REACH!ed for this? I decided to find out.

So I applied to Bentley along with a handful of other "safety" schools. Bentley was the *crème de la crème* of schools so I only half-heartedly believed that maybe I could get in. In fact, I didn't even think about whether I could balance that type of workload and a full-time job at the mortgage company (which I would again need to subsidize the cost).

Then, I got in—and not just to Bentley!

Sometimes when you really stretch and REACH! for something, not only does good news rain on you, it pours. The same day that I got my Bentley acceptance letter, I also received one from a competing university that also offered to give me a full scholarship to get my

Bachelor's degree. Bentley gave me the opportunity, but there would be no free ride. Choices, choices.

When you REACH!, you get the opportunity to make better choices. They are not necessarily *easy* choices, but they are higher-caliber choices for improving your life. Can you guess which school I went with? I was pretty much an expert on REACH!ing by this point, so I wasn't worried about balancing a full-time job and a full-time study at Bentley. This was my dream, and I had every intention on REACH!ing for it. So Bentley it was!

A few weeks later, I received my Associate's degree. I asked my mom and dad to postpone my graduation party and instead give me the money they would have spent on it so that I could get a laptop computer—my first ever. Having one was mandatory for Bentley students and I didn't want to borrow one. Besides, what seemed like such a huge milestone two years ago, getting an Associate's degree, seemed so small compared to what was possible now. I didn't see the need to celebrate.

Bentley would not transfer most of my community college credits, which meant I had to attend for three full years rather than two, but I did it. I didn't sail through like some kids. I worked day and night. If I wasn't at work or school, I was home studying. I enjoyed the hectic pace of work, school, work, school… But even more I enjoyed the thought that the effort I was making wasn't just about earning a degree. The hard work and stress I was experiencing was the result of REACH!. I was widening my possibilities and pulling my dreams closer. Not just one single dream, but all of them. In fact I was beginning to realize that *any* dream I could dream up was mine for the taking. REACH!ing is about stretching so far it hurts, getting outside of your comfort zone, and creating opportunity where there was none before.

While attending Bentley, I needed to make more money to pay for books and higher tuition—and to set aside savings. To do this, I needed a better job than copy girl. I approached my boss and asked for a job processing files. I had already learned how to do it on my own and I promised to be the best processor the company ever had. My boss was concerned that I could only work nights, but she reluctantly gave me the job and I fulfilled my promise: I was the best processor they'd ever seen. It was never unusual for someone to ride by the office at nine o'clock at night and see me working on files.

One of the great things about seizing opportunities, like a new job, is that it gives you even more great opportunities to REACH! further. For instance, had I not been given the opportunity to process loans, I may have never seen that other people just like me were making big bucks buying and selling investment properties. If they could do it, why not me? That's why in my first year at Bentley, I added one more job to my already busy schedule: property investor. There was a loan officer in my office who was successful at flipping properties and I wanted to learn all that he knew. Armed with the money I'd saved, my perfect credit score, my ever-growing ambition, and a willing mentor, I was soon actively buying, remodeling, and selling, investment real estate. This made it much easier to pay for school.

Three years later, I graduated from Bentley with a Bachelor's in accounting, and I still look back on my entire college career as formative years. It wasn't about the individual lesson plans I absorbed while sitting in class; it was more about learning to REACH! for opportunities that presented themselves throughout my time there. I was so lucky to be so young and to have learned the most important and valuable lesson I have ever learned:

I can be, do, and have anything in the world I want. I just have to be willing to REACH!!

Since I first applied to community college in 1990, I have spent more than twenty years now REACH!ing. I REACH!ed out and built a real estate empire in Massachusetts. I REACH!ed for and completed my first marathon two years ago. I REACH!ed out and met the love of my life and started a family very late in life. I REACH!ed for and acquired a law degree, and the ability to author several books. I achieved every remarkable breakthrough in my life because I REACH!ed for it. I didn't *Lean In* because I didn't have anything to lean in *to*. I created the opportunities and then REACH!ed, often blindly into the unknown, for the seemingly impossible.

Think you can't do it? I know you can. I've never met anyone who didn't possess a little bit of REACH!.

I should also take a moment to mention that this book isn't just for women, nor is it geared toward men. This book is for anyone with a burning desire within to accomplish a dream. I don't care how old you are, what color you are, what sex, race, religion, creed, or nationality. If there's something you want, anything at all, then REACH! was written for you.

This book is only taking me a day to write, which means it should only take you a day or two to read. I designed it that way. REACH! is the book to grab while watching your son or daughter's soccer practice. REACH! is the book to pull out of your purse in the dentist's waiting room. REACH! is absolutely that book you pull out when you are at a crossroads facing a difficult decision about moving or staying put. REACH! is about stretching outside your comfort zone because only then can you be, do, and have anything you put your mind to—and I mean *anything*.

Go ahead, you can do it. REACH!!

REACH! Challenge

1. Create your REACH! goals. Make a list of ten
   things you would do anything to accomplish in your
   lifetime. Do not limit yourself. Be unreasonable
   here! Assume that you can be, do, and have anything
   in the world you want, and create your list. This
   challenge is about REACH! so the items on this
   list should make you uncomfortable, and some
   should seem impossible. Dream big, stretch your
   imagination, get ready to achieve. You are about to
   REACH!.

   *Visit www.REACHTools.net for free
   downloadable REACH! resources.*

Chapter 3

Attitude Isn't Everything...

"Glory lies in the attempt to reach one's goal and not in reaching it."
– Mahatma Gandhi

Attitude isn't everything; it's the *only* thing.

If your attitude sucks, you will have very little REACH!. People won't like you, which means they won't converse with you. When people aren't conversing with you, you can't influence them or gain access to their knowledge or REACH!. When that's the case, you're stuck right where you started.

A bad attitude is usually grounded in what happened before today. I cannot control what happened yesterday. Neither can you. We all have had awful, gut-wrenching, do-not-repeat yesterdays. The absolute worst thing you can do is repeat yesterday—and I know you agree. And yet so many people repeat horrible yesterdays every day by dwelling on them in their own heads and even rehashing them out loud. Forget it. Drop it. Let it go. Make yourself stop thinking about it.

Are you good? Ok. Now you're on the path toward having an amazing attitude. And here's more good news: People with amazing attitudes about everything, always, always, *always*, have amazing REACH!. Why is that?

Well, for starters, people like happy people. If you have a choice between hanging out with Eeyore or Tigger from *Winnie the Pooh*, which would you choose? Sure, Tigger can be annoying because he doesn't stop bouncing. He's always happy and excited and jumping up and down. The alternative though, is a woe-is-me donkey who can't seem to enjoy anything he's doing and assumes the worst will happen in every situation.

We all have an Eeyore in our lives, don't we? What do you do when Eeyore calls you? Do you take his call right away? Or do you let it go to voicemail? "Oh, Eeyore wants to catch the game on Saturday with me? Um, I have to clean my gutters." You get where I am going, I'm sure. The big question here is: How much REACH! does Eeyore have at all? Eeyore is not REACH!ing for anything in his own life, besides you. And REACH!ing back out to Eeyore is not going to help you REACH! toward your own goals, be they happiness today or long-term success. Eeyore's a good enough guy, but really, we want to hang with Tigger.

What big life goal are you working on right now? Oh, you have a lifelong dream of starting your own indoor ice skating rink? Guess who is totally off-the-wall exuberant about that? Tigger! He is so freaking excited he can't stop bouncing! He totally sees your dream as if it is his own. In fact, Tigger knows people who can help you! He knows a guy who knows a guy who is selling a used Zamboni machine for really cheap. He also has a friend who does commercial real estate and has the perfect spot for an indoor rink. Tigger has a friend who sells ice skates, and another who runs a concession stand, and another who teaches ice skating lessons in the winter and would love to teach at your rink.

How does Tigger know all these people? How did he expand his REACH! so wide? Easy! Attitude. A great attitude is like a magnet. People want to be around other people with great attitudes. If you have a friend who is a Tigger, you are in luck because that person has got REACH!. You are probably one degree away from thousands, hundreds of thousands, or even millions of people because Tigger has REACH!. In fact, the only thing better than having Tiggers in your life… is being Tigger.

My good friend and business partner Christi is a Tigger. Every once in a while, you can catch her in a down mood, but you're more likely to catch a glimpse of Halley's Comet. She makes a concerted effort to be happy every day. She finds the good, happy, and positive in everything. She has a million friends. If I were going to open an indoor ice skating rink, I would call Christi first because she has REACH! over so many people it's almost unheard of.

A year ago, Christi gave birth to her third child, Michael, a beautiful baby boy diagnosed with Down syndrome. While many people in her situation might ask the universe, "Why my child?" or even "Why me," Christi literally threw her hands in the air and said, "Thank you, thank you, *thank you* for blessing me with this amazing child!" She talks about how blessed she is to have Michael (and her other children) at every event and fashion show she speaks at. If you are lucky, you will one day get to attend one and hear her yourself.

I also went through some health scares with my own young daughter, and there were many sleepless nights when I asked the universe, "Why me?" I know I have a tiny bit of Eeyore in me—nearly all of us do. But Christi recognizes that Michael brings out the best qualities in her, and the best in everyone else around him too. This is really important here, because I'm about to show you the impact—the immense REACH!—that a one-year-old child can have. (And if an infant can achieve this kind of REACH!, so can the rest of us.)

Christi will be the first to tell you that Michael is the creator of better people. He is smiley, cuddly, always happy, and makes others around him feel the same way. This kid is a born Tigger, and he's too young yet to even realize it. His infectious smile creates more Tiggers, even out of Eeyores. Christi and her family treat Michael no differently than any of their other kids, or than anyone else on earth. They see that Michael has the advantage not a disadvantage. He's the superhero. If you were mom or dad to little Clark Kent, would you treat him differently knowing that he's Superman? You wouldn't need to because he's already got the advantage and he doesn't need you to give him any more of it. So it is true with baby Michael, a born superhero, with the power to turn you into Tigger. The only power better than the ability to leap tall buildings in a single bound is the ability to transform someone's attitude. Superman can't do that, but Michael can. Now that's REACH!.

Life is not always easy; I get it. Sometimes really tough stuff happens that we have no control over. People with REACH!—the Tiggers of the world—turn these awful yesterdays into better tomorrows. My close friend Michelle is another shining example of how to REACH! through and beyond adversity. Michelle lost her teenage son, Luis, several years ago to appendicitis. It was heart-wrenching to watch her bear the pain of that loss. There wasn't much anyone could do to help her other than REACH! out and offer support. REACH! requires a concerted focus on tomorrow, rather than yesterday. We cannot change yesterday. We cannot bring back our lost loved ones. We can, however, control today and tomorrow.

Today, Michelle is a successful real estate agent and founder of the S.I.T.O. Foundation ("SITO" was one of Luis' nicknames, and stands for Strive Intelligence Through Originality). The foundation provides scholarships to help kids exiting trade school pay for postsecondary education or the physical tools needed for the trade they are entering. I have had the distinct pleasure of watching Michelle hand out these scholarships at graduations and witnessing the power of her REACH!. It includes every student she helps start a brighter future armed with the tools or classes they all need to succeed. She is truly changing lives in honor of her lost son.

Michelle has also created REACH! within her community because people are magnetized to her positive attitude and commitment to taking something so tragic and turning it into a better tomorrow for those around her. It's no wonder that Michelle has such a successful real estate business through which she helps forty or more families a year capitalize on the American Dream of homeownership. Families trust her because she has demonstrated her trustworthiness by giving back to local children who need a hand up upon entering or graduating from trade school. Michelle didn't REACH! out to her community for the purpose of making a profit; her goal was to help kids like her son Luis. But nevertheless, the REACH! she created within the community offered a drastic upside to her real estate business. REACH! does that. When you REACH! out to help your community, it tends to REACH! back to help you build a successful business.

Recently I had the distinct pleasure of doing a live interview with my mentor Dave Liniger. He is co-founder and board chairman of

RE/MAX and author of *My Next Step*, a story of how he almost lost his life in 2012 and was forced to learn how to walk again. Up until the start of 2012, Dave was usually traveling the world to further strengthen the foothold RE/MAX has had in the global real estate market. Early that year, Dave was in Texas preparing to speak to a large audience of RE/MAX agents and owners. He wasn't feeling great and was concerned his back was going to give out. So he notified his executive team to come look for him in his room in the morning if he didn't show up to breakfast.

Dave never did make it to breakfast because when he woke up early that morning, he couldn't move. He was paralyzed from the waist down. When his team found him in his room, they immediately called 911. He was rushed to a local hospital where he was told he would need surgery. He requested a transfer to a hospital in his own home state of Colorado. But within days of arriving in Denver, he slipped into a coma. It took several days and a series of operations to learn that Dave had suffered a serious staph infection from a light fall he had in his garage weeks earlier. That staph infection nearly killed him.

The number one attribute that got him through his tragedy was attitude. I would even go so far as to say that anyone with less absolute determination, unbridled will, and REACH! than he has would have spent the remainder of his or her life in a wheelchair. Dave's doctors told him he'd probably never walk again and that he should simply be grateful that he beat the odds and survived his ordeal. He was actually *encouraged* to face the reality of life in a wheelchair. But he did no such thing. He harnessed every bit of REACH! he had within him to take back his old life once again.

You heard right. Recovering from a weeks-long coma requires REACH!. Recovering from paralysis from the waist down requires it as well. It helps to REACH! out to others, of course. But first and foremost, you have to REACH! deep within yourself for the courage and will to live. Dave found that courage and will. Once he did that, he simply REACH!ed one foot in front of the other slowly, steadily, and with the constant support of medical staff, machines, and loved ones. Less than one year later, he was able to walk on his own again. Shortly after, he was back to running RE/MAX and still is today, feeling stronger than ever.

If you suddenly have to face adversity and don't have the attitude and REACH! required to overcome it, that doesn't mean you have to succumb. What you need, quite simply, is an attitude adjustment. Now before you say, "Easier said than done," let's look together at how easily it can be done.

Giving yourself an attitude adjustment takes three simple steps. I call them my PSG: Perspective, Smile, Gratitude.

1. **Perspective**

Whenever I need an attitude shift, it's usually because I have lost perspective. Three years ago, I lost my brother-in-law and great friend Ed Quinlan to ALS, also known as Lou Gehrig's disease. He was fifty years old with a wife and four children. I wouldn't wish ALS on my worst enemy. In less than four years, Ed deteriorated from a healthy, vibrant man coaching his kid's soccer team to living in a nursing home and unable to move any part of his body. I visited him each day in that nursing home. Since there is still no cure for ALS, Ed couldn't REACH! out or within for the resources to beat it and survive. But he continued to REACH! the family and friends who visited him, giving them all the love and attention he had left to give. And he also gave me the gift of perspective. I think about him often, and reflect upon his struggle whenever my issues (which thankfully pale in comparison) seem too great for me to handle.

Is today really that bad? So you're stuck in traffic, it's raining, you're late, you spilled coffee on your new suit, and the heel of your shoe broke off. There are worst things. No matter what kind of bad day you're having, it's not ALS. And that's what perspective is all about: being thankful for what you have (and, for that matter, what you don't have) and focusing on positively affecting things within your control. Instead of wasting even a millisecond feeling bad for yourself, take that moment and say a prayer for someone who has real problems that you don't.

And even if your problems *are* as bad as they get, you can still REACH! just like Ed did. Stephen Hawking, the English theoretical physicist, cosmologist, author, and research director at University of Cambridge's Centre for Theoretical Cosmology, has been living with ALS for more than forty years. Though confined to a wheelchair and unable to speak on his own, he has spent his life writing books, teaching, researching, and receiving some highly regarded accolades along the way including the Presidential Medal of Freedom, the Copley Medal, the Wolf Prize in Physics, and the Albert Einstein Medal, to name a few. Hawking shares his thoughts about ALS as well as his thoughts on black holes, the Big Bang Theory, and more on his website (www.Hawking.org.uk).

Hawking has also married twice and raised three children. He works, travels, and even takes on speaking engagements in front of large audiences with the help of a voice transmitter. This is a guy with all kinds of REACH!. Physically incapacitated for more than half his life, he continues to dream, stretch, achieve, and influence millions. If you guessed that Hawking has an extraordinary attitude and sense of perspective about his disease, you guessed right. He actually considers himself a pretty lucky guy. It doesn't take a lot of REACH! to put your own problems in perspective. If you're still breathing, you have the power to move forward.

Recently I attended an event keynoted by Chad Hymas, a motivational speaker and author of *Doing What Must Be Done*. Chad is also wheelchair bound after a fall paralyzed him in 2001. Though he cannot walk, he manages to travel the world speaking at more than two hundred events each year. When I heard Chad speak, he talked about the power of perspective. He asked an audience member to rate the importance of having hands on a scale of 1–10 with "10" being most important. The audience member replied that his hands would be a "10." Chad then asked the audience member how important his hands would be if he had to choose between having his hands or his eyesight; suddenly the hands dropped down to a "1." Nobody would want to live without hands, but probably most people would give up their hands in favor of keeping their eyesight. That's perspective.

Hymas noted that too often, people concentrate on what they don't have rather than what they do have. Perspective is about embracing the blessings you have while mentally letting go of those that you don't. For the first five years after Chad's accident, he was bitter, angry, and withdrawn because he dwelled on what he didn't have, mainly his ability to walk. But once he began to spend his energy on what he did still possess—his ability to get around, speak, see, and love—he built a brand new life for himself. It is this very perspective that has enabled Chad to create awesome REACH! among the audiences he educates worldwide.

2. Smile

If you smile while you're feeling negative, your inner emotions will actually turn from negative to positive. That is a scientific fact shared by Dale Carnegie in his 1936 book *How to Win Friends & Influence*

People. If you don't believe me, try it yourself. Smile all day and you will be a happier person for it. Not to mention, your smile will attract the attention of others who are smiling around you, and encourage those who aren't smiling to start. Therefore, the environment around you will become happier simply because of the small choice you made in yourself. So when my attitude is taking me to places I don't want to go, I simply smile and immediately begin to feel better.

My friend and business partner Ann Marie has talked often about her father-in-law Tim who was diagnosed in his twenties with type 1 diabetes. Despite always following his doctor's orders closely, Tim ended up losing his eyesight as result of his disease by his early fifties. The disease also compromised the circulation in his legs and kidneys resulting in two leg amputations and dialysis treatments four hours a day, three times a week. But throughout his trials and tribulations, Tim never complained. He always smiled and concentrated on the bright side of things. He was known as a jokester among his doctors and nurses. His attitude was always positive and inspiring, and he received great joy from just being with his wife, sons, and grandkids. Tim's REACH! to keep going was truly remarkable. His smile and attitude were contagious which is likely why his wife of forty years has said that despite the constant caretaking and hardships, she'd rather be with him every day than anywhere else. Smiling through life, no matter what it throws you, will improve your attitude and that of those around you.

3. Gratitude

Last, but certainly not least, you need to focus on gratitude in order to successfully shift your attitude. I take time every single day to thank the universe for my tons of blessings. Even when I lost everything I owned when the real estate market tanked in 2005, I remained grateful for my health, my friendships, and the roof over my head. I was grateful to have money for food. I was grateful that I could get free books to read at the library to keep my focus positive. I have always remained grateful for what I have, and I tend to spend very little time focusing on what I don't have.

Gratitude goes hand in hand with appreciation, which helps you create massive REACH! in your life. Today, take a moment to take stock in your inventory of relationships. I bet you have some pretty important people in your life, some who have stuck by you through thick and thin. Pick up the phone and say "Thanks," and let those important people know how much they mean to you. Whether you are at a high point, at rock bottom, or coasting along somewhere in the middle, you have people who support you. REACH! out to them and let them know you appreciate them.

Think back to the last time someone appreciated you. Maybe it was a friend who was grateful for your support in a tough time. Perhaps it was a customer. Sometimes appreciation comes from the strangest of places, like an ex-spouse, a neighbor, an employee, or a complete stranger. How did you feel when they expressed that appreciation? Pretty good, right? Do you kind of wish you could REACH! back and do even more for them because they appreciated you? People will feel the same way toward you when you show appreciation as well. Nothing lifts ones spirits like a little dose of gratitude. Go ahead, give some out, and there's no stopping your REACH!.

Here are three things you should *not* do when it comes to attitude:

1. Don't let others affect your attitude unless they are doing so for the better.

2. Don't accept other's opinions of you, unless they are good ones.

3. Don't—I repeat, *do not*—let others bring you down.

Remember that REACH! goes both ways. When you have the ability to REACH! others, you have the power to influence them positively *or negatively*. Eeyore does have some REACH! whether we like it or not. He absolutely does not have the REACH! that Tigger has, but he's got some nonetheless. Don't let his negative REACH! affect yours. It is imperative that you keep your own attitude in check in order to maintain your high level of positive REACH!. To do so will require you to mentally shut out those who try to bring you down.

A great example of someone who knows how to deflect bad energy and keep in the good is my friend Christina. Growing up, Christina was always the "fat kid," the one most people made fun of—or as she recalls it, tortured. In an effort to help Christina stave off obesity, doctors put her on a 600-calorie-a-day diet—at age 6. But no matter what diet or exercise she tried, she kept getting bigger and bigger. She eventually spiraled out of control in her mid-twenties and ballooned to over 250 pounds, then 300. She says that what she mostly felt was panic over the inability to control her own body. To deflect mean comments as a kid, she always tried to laugh them off and wore a smile on her face, even though she felt like she was dying inside. From an early age, she had learned to be stoic, resilient, and self-reliant. Christina thought that if she could wipe away her emotions on the outside, her actual emotions on the inside would follow suit—and sometimes they did. She stopped trying to play with the other kids so they couldn't reject her. As a result, other kids would form their own playground friendships and focus less on her, offering her the feeling of invisibility. There are some advantages to building such walls: By warding off other kids' negative energy, Christina was able to focus more on being an above-average student. In later years she would graduate college summa cum laude with a 3.9 grade point average. All the same, her obesity remained a detriment to her confidence, her ability to REACH!, and her health—and she was determined to do something about it.

In January 2003, Christina made the decision to seek out gastric bypass surgery options. Her primary care doctor referred her to a top local surgeon who helped develop the procedure. Christina was cleared to have the surgery and didn't ask anyone else if she should have it or not. She made the decision and that was it.

She had done the same thing when she bought her first condo; she told no one she was doing it until she closed on it. In both instances, she knew she was making the right decision and didn't need to hear other people's opinions. Reflecting back on both, she told me she was never scared, only extremely excited to make these significant positive changes in her life.

Christina had her surgery in July 2003. Over the next eighteen months, she lost half of her body weight. She says the transformation was surreal. Neighbors in her condo building would look at her in the elevator and say, "Something's different about you. Did you change your hair?" Christina was shocked. She had lost more than one hundred fifty pounds and people thought her big change was her haircut. She soon realized that she was the only one obsessed with her weight and that adults weren't as focused on it as the cruel kids on her childhood playground. Most likely, people were noticing Christina because as the weight came off pound by pound, her confidence levels grew. She walked proudly, beamed with enthusiasm, and looked people in the eye. What was different about Christina was the positive aura that she radiated as she tackled life with a new level of self-assuredness.

What if Christina had told people about her surgery before she had it? What if they had advised against it and she had listened to them? She might have let someone convince her not to REACH! for a positive life-altering change. There will always be naysayers who don't want you to REACH! because it makes *them* feel uncomfortable. If you're REACH!ing to achieve your greatest dreams, you should surround yourself with only positive energy. While it's always helpful to have a wide support network behind you, sometimes the best way to ensure a positive network is to keep it small—or even REACH! alone. In Christina's case, she was confident that her research, her own will power, and her medical team were all she needed to do the right thing for her. And looking back, she says it's the best thing she's ever done.

Christina's story doesn't end with a beautiful new attitude and figure—it gets better.

At the time of Christina's surgery, she was working for General Electric as a lead project manager, handling some of its largest New England projects. She liked her job but wanted to be more involved in management. Specifically, she had her eye on the operations manager position currently held by Bob, a cranky old man who was retiring in the next year. One day, Christina took it upon herself to REACH! out and knock on Bob's door. She asked if there was anything she could do to help him. And guess what? His face lit up. In Bob's forty-plus years at GE, no one had ever volunteered to help him with anything. He gave Christina project after project, always showing her what to do and how. And once she mastered a new skill, he'd help her develop another. With every new project, Bob was grooming Christina to take over once he retired.

Christina had laid some great groundwork for obtaining this exciting position. But even when you REACH!, things don't always go your way. That's why it's so important to have your attitude in check. GE policy dictated that when Bob's job was available, they had to post the job and give everyone a fair crack at the position. By the time Bob retired, a new branch manager had transferred from Naperville, Illinois, to oversee Christina and hire the next operations manager. Having no idea about Christina's talents, he brought in a newbie from Naperville to take the job even though he was far less qualified for the position. Adding insult to injury, Christina's boss asked her to train this new employee for the job *she* had been groomed for. REACH! was required.

Christina got up her courage, walked into her boss's office, and asked to be reconsidered for Bob's position since she was already trained to do it. Her boss asked her why and she explained that she had worked in the industry for more than ten years and recently put herself through full-time night school at Northeastern University, graduating with honors, while excelling at her position. She also told him that Bob had trained her on every aspect of the manager job and that over her ten years at GE, she had mastered every job in the organization from assembly line worker to CEO.

At this point, her boss stopped her mid-sentence, leaned toward her, and said, "Christina, you will NEVER earn $100,000 a year." When she heard that, she had two clear choices: Resign herself to working under a boss who had no interest in developing her skills or career; or REACH! for a different path toward advancement. Christina chose the latter and immediately signed up for real estate school weeks later.

Christina passed her salesperson test in December 2003. Two years later Christina was one of the most successful real estate agents in her firm, earning over $500,000 per year. So I guess her old boss was right; Christina would never earn $100,000 a year—she skipped right past that figure and now earns several times more. Today she runs her personal real estate sales business along with several other businesses. She runs them from her home in Hawaii. And it all started with someone telling her "No," and her decision to REACH! above it.

REACH! Challenge

1. WWTD? (What would *Tigger* do?) List five things that you have had a less-than-positive attitude about in your life. Find the silver lining in each situation and commit to switching to this new positive attitude when you reflect on the situation.

2. Refer back to your REACH! goals from Chapter 2. For each goal, list out the tools you have to achieve this goal with. Rather than reflect upon what you *don't* have, redirect your focus to what you *do* have. We will build your artillery in further chapters. But for now, realize that you are armed with significant tools to achieve.

Visit www.REACHTools.net for free downloadable REACH! resources.

Chapter 4
Network

"Funny thing how when you reach out, people tend to reach right back. Best, then, to make sure your hand is open and not fisted."
– *Richelle E. Goodrich*

You have probably heard before that you are the average of the five people you spend the most time with. This notion, written by entrepreneur and author Jim Rohn, is one of the most powerful notions you will need to embrace in order to create the life you want, build the business you always dreamed of, or accomplish any goal you put your mind to. The network of people you spend time with is absolutely vital.

In Todd Duncan's book, *Time Traps*, Duncan reminds us that how we spend our time deeply impacts every aspect of our lives including our self-esteem, identity, and sense of fulfillment. Thus, *whom* we spend our time with is as important as *how* we spend it. If you could pick any person in the world to be your closest friend, would you prefer: a) the person who has accomplished everything he or she has ever set out to do; or b) the person who plays video games all day because he or she would rather be lost in another world rather than contemplate a better future in this one?

Look closely at your friends, family, coworkers, and acquaintances. Are the people around you poised and ready to help you move closer to your big dreams? Are they your advocates? Are they high-fiving you and reminding you regularly, "You can do this," or are they holding you back? Surrounding yourself with an amazing support network is vital to achieving great things. You have the power to create your surroundings, attract your advocates, and choose your friends. So choose wisely.

In Darren Hardy's book, *The Compound Effect*, he talks about the phenomenon of pace. If you walk alongside someone who walks slowly, you will slow down your own pace to stay in step. If you walk alongside someone who walks quickly you will walk quickly.

How does this apply when it comes to the network of people you associate with? Well, if your business partner is really positive, outgoing, and charitable, you will show more of these qualities as well. If your closest friends all have happy, healthy relationships at home, there's a greater likelihood that you will as well. Remember how your mom used to freak out because you were hanging out with the wrong crowd in school? It's because your mom understood the phenomenon of pace. If your friends were lousy in school and partied all the time, your mom knew that you were more likely to end up like them.

I address network straightaway in this book because it's so important to achieving your life goals. There's a couple of ways I use the word network here and I use them interchangeably. First, your network is the people you influence in some way. It's the people who know you. Interestingly, you don't always know them, but they know you. I'm REACH!ing you right now and there's a good chance we have never met. Conversely, I have been personally influenced by the likes of Tony Robbins, Dale Carnegie, Napoleon Hill, and thousands of others, dead or alive, whom I have never met.

Second, network is a verb meaning "to create and strengthen relationships with those who influence you or visa versa." Networking is essential because it gives you the power to expand your REACH!. Think of it as increasing the speed of your Learjet.

I used to be the person who hated networking. There's nothing so awful as walking into a room full of people you don't know and standing around. Thankfully I've figured out a few ways to get past this. I had to, of course, and you can too.

How can you build a network even if you despise networking?

1. **Never let your fear or loathing of networking get in your way.** Networking is so important to my livelihood, and to yours, that it must be done at all costs. Therefore, find people who are doing what you want to do or people who can ultimately be a client for the business you want to create, and simply start talking with them.

2. **Be an active leader in groups that are really important to helping you achieve your goals.** Join a committee. This is the fastest way to get to know some of the other movers and shakers in your interest area faster and more deeply. These committee members probably know many contacts within the organization you want to REACH! and they have

the ability to make sure you are comfortable and confident talking with them. They are the ones you can flock to and ask for important introductions at events you attend.

3. **At least consider being the person who checks everyone in at events**. If you are too busy or not interested in joining a committee, this gives you the opportunity to learn everyone's names, introduce yourself, and select the ones you really want to hone in on later and get to know.

It is through networking organizations that I have developed some of my most cherished friendships. These are friends I would never have made had I not attended a networking event or joined a networking group. I have seen the impact of networking on my life and businesses. There were lots of times in my life when I felt like I was on the Titanic; I hadn't been paying attention, my life ran into a big iceberg, and I started to sink.

By the time I was twenty-six, I was a self-made millionaire. I was one of the most successful mortgage originators in my firm and I was fervently flipping real estate. Less than five years later, I had lost most everything I had, including my money, my first fiancé, and my hope that things would rebound. I have since regained everything I once had and then some. I did it by realizing that, even though my ship was sinking, there was something I still held firmly, and that was my network. I was sinking, but my REACH! was far and wide. I had impacted people's lives and had built strong relationships with peers inside and outside of my business, and they were there to help me regain what I had lost. There is amazing power in the people around you, so be thoughtful about whom you surround yourself with, and don't hesitate to REACH! whenever possible.

The power of your network enables you to multiply the power of your REACH! tenfold! I own a successful coaching and consulting firm known as P3 Coaching. I started it in 2010 with two amazing partners, Andy Armata and Jeff Wright. One of our areas of expertise is consulting clients who are entrepreneurs, small business owners, and salespeople. In 2011, I read a really good sales book, *The Seven Levels of Communication*, and wanted to share it with my clients. So I REACH!ed out to the author, Michael Maher, and asked if I could interview him about the book and post the interview on my blog. When he agreed, I had a better idea to do the interview live so that all my clients could hear it too. He agreed, and it went perfectly. My clients loved it and still listen to the recorded version of that interview today.

The whole experience taught me some valuable lessons in building REACH!. Of course, I expanded my own personal network by REACH!ing out to Michael, who is now a great personal friend of mine. But my customers all benefited from my REACH! as well. They were able to glean lessons and tips from a best-selling author and, in turn, viewed me as a more valuable resource for the information they need to succeed. All this resource sharing, all these newly developed tools for success, and all the added trust in me as a business consultant came from a single out-of-the-box idea and a phone call.

The interview with Michael Maher was so successful, I decided to REACH! further. I could do better than one interview with a best-selling author right? Of course I could. It just takes REACH!.

A month after Michael's interview, I grabbed another book off my bookshelf, *Selling Luxury Homes*, and contacted the author, Jack Cotton, for an interview. He said "Yes!" and my clients loved that one too. Plus Jack became another close personal friend of mine.

I had now established an interview series that helped expand my personal REACH! and my clients'. In two years, I've interviewed fifty or sixty amazing people with expertise in business, sales, entrepreneurship, life skills, business planning, marketing, and more. Darren Hardy, Stefan Swanepoel, Gary Vaynerchuk, Bob Beaudine, Nancy Michaels, Rob White, Marc Wayshak, Marilee Driscoll, Allison Maslan, Hugh Liddle… and the list goes on.

There's another person who learned about REACH! based on a single defining interview—his led to the greatest book of all time (in my opinion). His name was Napoleon Hill, author of *Think and Grow Rich*. Published in 1937, it is a timeless blueprint for creating financial wealth and for attracting what you want in life. The book grew out of an interview that he originally had with the wealthiest man in America at the time, Andrew Carnegie, while writing for *Bob Taylor's Magazine*, a popular magazine known for showing business people how to achieve power and wealth. Hill was compiling a story about wealthy individuals, which caused him to exercise his own REACH!. When he approached Carnegie for an interview, the seventy-three-year-old steel magnate propelled Hill's REACH! even further by commissioning Hill to interview more than five hundred of the richest men and women in the world so that he could write a comprehensive blueprint for individual success. You see, Hill did not have the access to REACH! these people on his own, but Andrew Carnegie was able—and willing—to help. The result was *Think and Grow Rich*, a book that sold twenty million copies by Hill's death, and more than seventy million today. And Hill owed it all to his REACH!, the power of multiples where networks shared amongst peers can create great things.

And don't forget—REACH! is not just for learning from others, but also for building an audience for your own expertise. In 2012,

I chaired an education committee for my local real estate board. Why would I sit on, let alone chair, this committee? As I said earlier, it gives me the ability to network with real estate agents from my own firm and other firms, and to form closer bonds with the movers and shakers in my area of expertise. After one particular committee meeting, the CEO of our board told me that an author named Marc Wayshak had REACH!ed out and sent us a copy of his book, *Game Plan Selling*, and asked to be considered as a speaker for an upcoming real estate event we were hosting. As committee chair, I was asked to read the book. I brought the book with me on my Martha's Vineyard vacation and, boy, did I love it. Based on my swift recommendation, the real estate board invited Marc to be our keynote speaker.

For most, that might be a good enough ending to that story. But "good enough" is never good enough when you want to REACH!. One key to REACH!: Always be looking for ways to expand it. For me, just having Marc speak at that event was not going to be good enough. I wanted to create more REACH! for Marc and myself. So I invited him to do a live webinar with me and present the ideas in his book to my consulting client base, which he did. Like all my other interviews, it was very well received. My clients were so appreciative of me for bringing Marc to them that I created even greater loyalty amongst my client base.

Meanwhile, Marc and I got to talking afterward about how he published his book and how he runs his own consulting business, and we decided to talk more over lunch. While at lunch he invited me to a Saturday meeting of a group called The New England Speakers Association. I went to that Saturday's meeting and have not missed one since. For someone like me, being introduced to a group of other speakers, consultants, and coaches was a dream come true. By inviting me to this group, Marc expanded his REACH! to me and brought me into a new organization with a whole new vantage point on a business that I totally love.

It is from this group that I formed three amazing friendships: Marc, Marilee Driscoll, and Nancy Michaels. All three are extremely accomplished authors and speakers who together invited me into a separate monthly mastermind group with them. We meet monthly to discuss ideas, techniques, and strategies for building businesses. The three of them are so far ahead of me in their accomplishments as authors and speakers that I just shut my mouth sometimes and hope they don't realize I'm the odd one in the group. But if they've ever thought that, they haven't let on. Instead, we all share our ideas equally. We share our networks. We share our REACH!. And for that, I am grateful.

By the way, I mentioned that I share my interviews with my clients. Well I also share many of my interviews with *potential* clients. If you are growing any type of business, then you probably need clients. And one great way to attract potential clients and prove your value to them is to demonstrate your REACH!. I do this by sharing my older interviews with possible clients through my blog. If you visit my website (www.staceyalcorn.com), you can listen to full interviews with some of the authors I've met. It's my way of showing potential clients that if you want to grow your business, I can help by giving you access to the most amazing visionaries, writers, and experts of all time.

Blogging is another way you can create greater REACH! and use it to further credential yourself among current and potential clients. By writing regularly for several blogs including *The Huffington Post*, I get the opportunity to impact people I've never met. These people weren't seeking out the latest content from Stacey Alcorn; they happened to find me while reading a well-known outlet. If someone is reading your blog then you are reaching them, and that alone is powerful stuff.

A blog is a great and inexpensive way to REACH! your networks, whether it's through *Huffington* or your own free site. Four years prior to becoming a *Huffington* writer, I started my own personal blog, using a free Wordpress site. I still blog on it today and have since expanded to additional blogs including one for my consulting firm, one for my real estate company, and one for my fashion business.

A third method for expanding your REACH! is asking your network members to introduce or refer you to broad groups or specific individuals you want to meet. Who do I know that you need to know? If you can make a link between two people, then you have created REACH! that benefits everyone. Social media makes linking people easier than ever. Social tools like LinkedIn, Facebook, and other online sites give you the ability to quickly scan through your connections and determine which people would benefit from knowing one another.

I am such an avid believer in the power of networking that I pay big money to be included in the groups and organizations that offer me extended REACH!. Last year I was offered the opportunity to attend an invitation-only High Performance Forum hosted by *Success Magazine's* Darren Hardy. Three times a year, Darren brings together a group of twenty-five CEOs and shares his blueprint for success. Darren, a modern day Napoleon Hill, has personally interviewed all of the most successful people in the world. So of course I want to be in his High Performance Forum and rub shoulders with those he considers good company!

When I heard the price of attending Darren's Forum, I nearly choked. Then I consider the cost-benefit of REACH!ing into my pocket, as it were. Not only would I get the opportunity to learn from the one individual alive today who has built a blueprint of success based on the experiences of all the world's most successful people, but also I was getting the rare opportunity to spend three glorious days with twenty-four other high-caliber CEOs, entrepreneurs, authors, coaches, speakers, and experts who each have just as much to teach—and their own REACH!es that they could potentially share with me. Is there such thing as an ROI on REACH!? I can tell you with absolute certainty: *Yes*.

I invested in my REACH! by attending Darren Hardy's High Performance Forum and let's just say that the return on that investment thus far has been far greater than that of any other investments I have made.

Or course, access to high-power organizations isn't just for those with big money. There are plenty of ways you can be the one to galvanize your own CEO networking groups in your community. Find the people you want to connect with and organize a high-powered executive breakfast once a quarter to share ideas and build off one another's knowledge. Make sure you are armed with great content for helping your group grow, stick to an agenda, and start and finish on time. High-powered executives will respect you if you respect their time.

Perhaps CEOs are not the people you want to target. Identify the type of people you want to network with and build from there. Find those people in your markets, REACH! for them, and bring them together for a common purpose: to learn and share ideas.

Pamela Ryckman wrote a fantastic book called *The Stiletto Network* about women's groups around the world that support and promote each other's successes and achievements. These are merely groups of girlfriends that network regularly and share their REACH! by exposing one another to the people they know and influence. There are thousands of networking groups out there, and all of them require just a little REACH! to be part of them or to start your own. Choose your network wisely because these friends and advocates have the power to take your REACH! to whole new levels.

I have grown several incredibly powerful networks among Realtors, philanthropists, public speakers, writers, CEOs, and more. They have all helped expand and strengthen my REACH!. And the greater the REACH! of both myself and those around me, the more we want to be in one another's company. REACH! truly leads to more REACH!.

If you are not where you wish to be in your life, take a look at your REACH! and how you can expand it in a way that brings you closer to the life you desire. Get involved in new networks. Get yourself vested in a group of people who are as good or better than you at something you want to be really good at. If you are apprehensive about working a room, join a committee. It's a great way to hear from others and then contribute your own strengths at your pace. Do these things and I promise you that before long, you will have the REACH! you need to REACH! higher.

REACH! Challenge

1. Review your list of REACH! goals from Chapter 2. For each goal listed, write down three networks you should belong to that would help you achieve that goal. Networks may include trade groups, charitable organizations, community groups, business networking groups, and social assemblies.

2. Not sure which networks to get involved with? Find individuals who are already REACH!ing for the same or similar goals and ask them what groups they recommend you be involved in.

3. Once you examine your list, choose two networks to join immediately. Don't overcommit! Joining too many groups too soon may result in a saturated schedule. Join networks that will further your most important REACH! goals.

4. Upon selecting a network to join, volunteer for a committee. This will result in the quickest possible saturation into the network, helping you begin the process of forming important relationships that will enable your REACH!.

Visit www.REACHTools.net for free downloadable REACH! resources.

Chapter 5

Kids

"It's not only children who grow. Parents do too. As much as we watch to see what our children do with their lives, they are watching us to see what we do with ours. I can't tell my children to reach for the sun. All I can do is reach for it myself." – Joyce Maynard

Where does REACH! come from? Are some people born with a certain genetic chemistry that gives them the ability to create audacious goals and then achieve them? Perhaps some are genetically disposed to risk taking so they are more likely to achieve? Are we doing a disservice to our children by not offering them real world tools to REACH! for whatever they desire in life? In this chapter we talk about the power of REACH! in children, how to create it, and how you can encourage it. This is about teaching kids the power of achievement and building a network.

According to one UCLA study, the average toddler hears the word "no" four hundred times a day. We often tell them that to protect them from harm. We want them to understand the risk of talking to strangers, jumping from high places, and touching hot stoves. Our "nos" are helpful in that regard. However, the unattended side effect of four hundred "nos" a day is that we prevent REACH! at an early age. More on this later.

Your REACH! and ability to REACH! are pivotal in helping you teach your children why and how to REACH! in their own lives so that they can envision and pursue their own dreams. REACH! is probably the most important practice you can instill in your children, yet it isn't something you can simply explain to them; you must demonstrate it daily by what you say and do.

Your kid is your "Mini-Me." You are creating a mini version of you that will someday walk, talk, and REACH! (or not REACH!) like you, unless he or she finds a greater influencer than you. Many children won't. Therefore, it's incumbent upon you to recognize the power of your REACH! over them. Kids who don't how to REACH! and create their own opportunities in life will not only struggle to properly envision and pursue their own goals, they also won't create the other kind of REACH!—being able to positively influence others, which would help them achieve these goals and build lasting positive relationships.

I am the only one in my family who flies. No, I don't have wings, or a pilot's license, but I do travel quite a bit around the world for speaking engagements. I grew up with my mother's fear of flying instilled in me, as did my brother and sister. Even to this day, my mother checks on the status of my will if I fly somewhere—to make sure she has rights to see my daughter when my plane plunges into the Atlantic ocean. I don't enjoy flying as much as others do, but at least I don't find it as excruciating as I once did. Don't get me wrong,

I don't think my mother ever *wanted* to instill this fear in my siblings and me, but she did nonetheless through her words and actions.

As a result of my mother's fear, we never traveled far on family vacations. When my baton-twirling troop went to Russia, I stayed behind because flying to another country was just beyond comprehension for my mother. Her justification was that we have everything we need right here in Massachusetts, so why risk life and limb to go somewhere else?

As I advanced in my career, I quickly realized that I couldn't REACH! for my big dreams while sitting in Massachusetts. Doing so would have severely limited my ability to REACH! for anything I wanted. So I stepped out of my lifelong comfort zone—something we all must do in order to truly REACH! for what we want. I've been flying regularly now for fifteen years. I attend conferences that enable me to grow. I network with people around the world. I speak to large organizations around the globe about the power of REACH!.

What if I had not reached outside of my limited beliefs about flying that my mother instilled in me? Where would I be today? Probably sitting in a mediocre office with a career that is less than fulfilling and a REACH! that only extended to the people I'd see daily at the office. That's why understanding your REACH! is so important as a parent. There's a chance that your kids will forever live within the boundaries you set and that they will later pass those down to future generations. So make sure those boundaries are as limitless as they can be, and encourage them to REACH! whenever possible.

My mother did teach me to develop wonderful habits as well. I am a dedicated mother to my three-year-old daughter Oshyn and I carve out a piece of every day that is just for her, just like my mother did for me. I also stick up for myself and others like my mother did. Naturally your kids will pick up many of your habits. Make sure they are good ones. Do your best not to instill fear or caution unless it's absolutely necessary. Remember that we all have the ability to instill greatness in our children.

How do you teach your kids to REACH!? The best way is to always demonstrate your own power and sincere desire to try something new. Try not to voice your own fears to your kids. For example, even if you don't like flying, happily get on the plane or encourage your child to fly away on a vacation with someone else—whom you wholly trust, of course. Demonstrate an openness to meeting new people, trying new foods, attending large events, public speaking— and encourage your children to be equally open to these experiences. When you feel fear, your child knows it, and you are instilling that same fear in his or her heart.

Also, be kind. The power of a kind word or gesture expands your REACH! because you will always inevitably find people who want to reciprocate that kindness. If you want to build a powerful network of advocates, be kind to people and you will create a team of people who want to help you accomplish your goals. Kindness can mean letting a car move ahead of you in busy traffic. Does that create REACH! right then and there? Probably not, but it doesn't suspend REACH!. The same is true if you let someone ahead of you in line at the supermarket. Kindness is making a plate of food for your neighbor who has been ill. It is raking leaves for your elderly friend. There are a million ways to practice kindness. Show me someone who practices it every single day, and I will show you someone who has major REACH!. Children who grow up to create REACH! through acts of kindness are often the product of parents who did the same.

So now we're encouraging our children to try new things and demonstrating kindness to them—but we're still saying "no" four hundred times a day. When you say no to your child, you are discouraging them to REACH! in the formative years of their lives. What if, when they were learning to walk, we said "No, no, no! Keep crawling!" We want them to walk. We want them to REACH!. We want them to live life unlimited, yet the message we often portray is one of caution and holding back. The trick is to help your children recognize when it's ok to REACH! and when to exercise caution.

I challenge you to carry around a piece of paper with you today. Mark a slash every time you tell your kid "NO." Do it for a few days and see how many times you discourage them from doing something. Then reflect. Were there any opportunities within those nos that you could have said, "Go for it"? I am suggesting that although it may be impossible to eliminate the word "no" when talking to your kids, *reducing* the number of times you say it may create that balance you are looking for.

I have done this exercise myself to see what the results would be. What I realized about myself is that many of the nos I was saying to my three-year-old daughter had nothing to do with keeping her safe; I was saying "no" because I was tired and worn out. In fact, I realized I was saying "no" way more late at night than in the morning. The word "no" had become the rote answer to so many questions when I should have been saying, "Go for it!"

So go ahead, give it a try. Teach your child to REACH!. It takes practice, no doubt. I still get tired and I still catch myself when I'm saying no for no good reason. By regularly taking the challenge, I'm offering my daughter a greater opportunity to REACH!,

How do we encourage kids to expand their other REACH!—the expanded network kind? Have parties with family and friends to show them the positive side of networking. Let your children try out lots of different social groups like the Girl or Boy Scouts, missionary work, team sports, theater, chess clubs, you name it. The power of every group is in the people found there and you should work diligently to support your children's ability to meet them whenever possible. Reinforce the bonds he or she builds with friends made in these groups by allowing extra time for them to bond further (i.e., day trips, sleepovers).

Also be sure to show your child the power of introductions. Being able to formally and eloquently introduce yourself to a stranger creates powerful REACH! by adding a new acquaintance *and* possibly getting to meet his or her connections in the future. Introducing two of your acquaintances who would otherwise be strangers is equally powerful; when you increase someone else's REACH!, they tend to want to increase yours too. Oftentimes our children end up forming long-term bonds with other kids we group them with when they are younger. We put them into playgroups where we create their REACH! for them. While this is a good thing, too often we forget to show them how to create REACH! on their own. When you offer your children lessons on how to break the ice in a room full of strangers and how to introduce two friends, you are offering your children a tool that they will carry with them for the rest of their lives.

Judgment is one negative characteristic that we often pass onto our kids, most times without even realizing it. I remember as a child that my mother would judge other kids I would play with. I would hear these judgments and wonder how she could know more about my friends than I did. I also wondered if the parents of my friends were judging me. I look back now and realize that my mom was trying to protect me. Her judging (and often misjudging) my friends was no different than her protecting me from burning myself on a hot stove. However, the implications of teaching a child to pass judgment are far reaching, a slippery slope if you will. REACH! requires acceptance of others and an appreciation for each individual's unique mix of personality, ideas, and history.

Forming a conclusion about others is something that we all do, often unintentionally and without malice. I've even done this myself by accident. One day I made a comment to my three-year-old about her friend down the street; I called him a jock because he's always playing a different sport outside. The comment was harmless and I meant nothing negative by it, but it's these quick, little judgments that can have monumental effects on the mind of a young child.

"What's wrong with a jock," she might wonder after hearing me label someone that. "Does that mean my mom doesn't want me to play sports?" When you pass judgment of any kind, you discourage REACH!, and nothing good can come from that. When we create labels for people, even innocent ones like "jock," we build barriers between us and people we could have otherwise REACH!ed out to. As parents, our goal should be to eliminate barriers for ourselves and teach our children to do the same—encouraging them to build friendships with a wide array of people. If you can find it within yourself to accept the virtues of everyone around you, your children will see that and likely do the same.

When it comes to REACH!, it is important to accept others and equally important to REACH! within ourselves to find love and acceptance for who we are. Anyone who knows me personally knows that I count calories and work out a lot. I am hard on myself when it comes to my health and my weight. Regardless the benefits of my self-motivation, being hard on yourself is not a good thing for your kid to see. I try never to say anything about myself in front of my daughter—good or bad—because if I did, I'd be encouraging her to pass similar judgment on herself.

The innate problem whenever we pass negative judgment on ourselves is that it lowers confidence—and confidence promotes REACH!! When I am confident, I have no problem going after what I want in life; but without it, it's not so easy. If you want your child to REACH! for what he or she wants, confidence is required. If you don't pass negative judgment on yourself, you will teach your kids not to do it either. And I can tell you for sure, you will all be a whole lot better for it.

In fact, we all benefit when we stop judging others. REACH!ing out to others with kind gestures instead of judging them from afar can help boost their confidence and produce positive auras all their own.

Remember my friend Christina? She enjoyed a major confidence boost after her successful gastric bypass surgery and losing more than half her body weight. Both men and women began to notice her more. People held doors open for her more often. And since she felt better about herself, she started spending more time pursuing things she wanted out of life instead of dwelling on her imperfections.

But what if Christina couldn't have afforded surgery? What if she was still struggling with her weight today? Perhaps the world would be a lot less bright for the lack of Christina's recently acquired REACH!. That is unless someone else came along and helped bring it out in her. Sure, Christina is responsible for her own confidence—but so am I. And you. And everyone around her. People are responsible for the wellbeing of one another—and equally benefit when each of us gains positive REACH!. It's not difficult to promote REACH!. Simple strides like a kind word, a smile, and even holding a door open for someone can create just the kind of REACH! that spreads like wildfire, creating a network of advocates, friendships, partners, and cheerleaders on the road to your dreams.

We all need to do a better job of being kind and accepting of those who are not like us. We need to make sure amazing people like Christina realize that they are beautiful—inside and out—and encourage them to share their amazing gifts with the rest of us in return. We all have the power to stop judging people—and to teach others to do the same. And who better to teach than our kids?

Kids are very perceptive. They pick up stuff that you don't even know you are putting down, as I like to say. My other friend and business partner Christi has a five-year-old daughter named Lily. She has beautiful blonde hair and is already quite the philanthropist.

Actually, I did it again. A compliment on Lily's hair is still a judgment based on appearance and has no affect on her characteristics. Allow me to start over…

Christi's daughter Lily is five years old and is already quite the philanthropist. When Lily found out her good friend Joey had been diagnosed with hypertrophic cardiomyopathy and was in need of a new heart, Lily went right to work raising money to help his family pay for his new heart and other hospital bills. She started by selling painted rocks for $1 at her family's farmstand and even to local businesses. When Christi shared Lily's creative idea on Facebook, sales went viral and more local businesses supported the idea by making large donations for one of Lily's painted rocks. This proves to me that Lily lives in a family environment where giving is the status quo. Five-year-olds don't naturally react to bad news by painting and selling rocks; that sort of giving spirit has to be learned. In this case,

Lily got it from her loving and giving parents. And when you both practice and preach philanthropy in your family, you should expect nothing less than raising a five-year-old philanthropist like Lily.

There are millions of stories of people who were influenced by their parents, guardians, older siblings, grandparents, aunts, or uncles. As well, there are many kids who didn't grow up with strong parental support but still achieve notable REACH! thanks to the positive influence of other mentors. Instilling positive REACH! in your children from the beginning will end up putting your kid on the path to creating his or her own positive REACH!.

REACH! Challenge

1. Count your nos. For the next twenty-four hours, count the number of times you say "no." Mark them down on a piece of paper and then tally them up at the end of the day. Are all of those nos 100 percent necessary? I challenge you to turn most of those nos into YESes!

2. Pull a YES out of thin air. There's a good chance that someone is going to ask you something today and is expecting you to say "no." Surprise them; tell them: "Go for it!"

3. Write down five fears you have. Next to each one, write down the source of that fear. Are you harboring trepidation passed on down to you from your parents? Is it possible that the foundation to your fear is weak? What small steps can you take to get past the fear altogether?

Visit www.REACHTools.net for free
downloadable REACH! resources.

Chapter 6

The Greatest Gift

"Love is a fruit in season at all times, and within reach of every hand."
— Mother Teresa

If you wake up every day and ask the world, "Whom shall I give to today," you will have absolutely no problem creating REACH! in your life. The fact is: Givers have greater REACH! than takers. This is because people shy away from takers. If you have ever had someone in your life who just takes, takes, takes, you know what I am talking about. You cringe when they call you. You delay opening their emails. Takers are not pleasant to be around. For that reason, people want to *help* givers more than takers. Therefore, if you dedicate your life to giving, then when you are ready to REACH! for your own goals, you will have no problem at all finding people who want to help you. So great givers actually create both types of REACH! for themselves: great connections, and positive influence over them.

Two of the greatest gifts my parents handed down to me were the power and the desire to give. Even though we were not wealthy by any means, my parents believed in giving to those in need. I remember taking a morning off from school every holiday season to ride into Boston with my dad and drop off toys for WBZ Radio's annual Toys for Tots toy drive. We always arrived with a station wagon full of Cabbage Patch dolls, Furskins, and other toys. It wasn't until later in life that I realized the impact this had on others. When you're young, you're told that you're helping others but you figure you're just helping Santa who is obviously going to take care of every kid regardless. Then one day you realize that your parents *are* Santa, not just for you, but also for other kids who weren't so lucky.

I mentioned earlier that achieving REACH! often means touching others whom you will likely never know. When you drop a toy in the Toys for Tots box, send a check to your favorite charity, or donate your clothing to The Salvation Army, all of these actions demonstrate your ability to cast out amazingly impactful REACH! into the universe. You change lives every time you cast your line. Your gifts impacts other lives, often increasing their confidence as they feel more valued by those around them. Sometimes, recipients of strangers' generosity feel so inspired by the power of a stranger's gift, they decide they should pay it forward and live a life dedicated to giving back themselves.

I was inspired by my parents to keep giving and I'm passing it down to my daughter. Every time Oshyn and I go grocery shopping, she picks out food for us to drop into the Food Pantry box that sits by the exit door. We also host a large-scale charitable event on Oshyn's birthday each year to collect toys for a local women's shelter. My lesson to her is that every December 11, the whole world celebrates her birthday with her because she's using it to make the world a better place. Her life has REACH! and she's only three years old.

Whenever I talk about the power of giving in my training programs or events, it's inevitable that someone will come up to me after and say, "I wish I could give but I just don't have the money." Giving is about so much more than money. In fact, giving something other than money—like your personal time—is *more* powerful than giving cash donations. Time is a limited commodity, while cash is boundless. When it comes to charities, most exist upon a delicate balance of people who donate money and others who donate time.

By the way, giving to a charity is wonderful, but this is such a small segment of your giving opportunity. When was the last time you visited a nursing home? Spend fifteen minutes with someone lonely and it's a far greater gift than dropping a monetary donation in the mail. You've given someone the gift of genuine personal connection. That person will feel the warmth of your REACH!—and even reciprocate it back to you. Now you're both giving and receiving, and that's a powerful thing worth enjoying. Volunteer one day a month at a food pantry and help fill a room with a spirit of giving that's greater than the sum of all the volunteers present. Be a Big Brother or Big Sister and help positively influence children who may not have others in their lives showing them how to create positive REACH!.

What do you do for work? Consider offering your services pro bono to an individual, group, or organization in your community or elsewhere that could benefit from them. Chances are you have a Rotary Club or other community action group in your town. If you are looking for people with REACH!, this is a good spot to find them. You will find a vast array of men and women

REACH!ing out within their community to provide time, money, and other support for the sake of improving the lives of those around them.

In my town, there's a woman named Patti whom I consider to be one of the town's most influential people. If you need anything at all, she has the entire town on speed dial and people will jump when she asks for something. Why? She created huge REACH! over time by volunteering for her Rotary Club, Habitat for Humanity, the local museum, and other organizations. With each activity, she meets more people who see all the good she's doing—and genuinely bond with her over their mutual passion for giving back. Patti is now retired and has dedicated herself full time to helping people and organizations that need her.

The REACH! that Patti has established for herself didn't cost her a penny, just her time and passion. And for all that, she's received so much more in communal love and friendship. If you have money and the desire to give it, then by all means do. But if you are not currently in a position to give money, then rest assured you don't need a dime to create REACH! through giving—just your time and positive energy.

I prefer to associate with givers. Wouldn't we all prefer that? Isn't it more rewarding to be surrounded by givers than takers? I seek out people who want to give and I do my best to give to them as a way of creating a larger spirit of goodwill.

On January 12, 2010, a horrible earthquake struck Haiti. More than 250,000 people lost their lives, including a girl by the name of Britney Gengel. She was from Massachusetts and had been in Haiti doing missionary work as part of a class she was taking at Lynn

University in Florida. Minutes before the earthquake, Britney sent her parents a text message about how the people of Haiti were so positive and grateful for their blessings, even though they had so little, and that Britney wished to come back again some day and build an orphanage for the children of Haiti. Less than a few hours later, Britney perished in the earthquake.

In the aftermath of that horrendous day, Britney's parents Len and Cherylann Gengel vowed to turn their loss and grief into something positive—they vowed to carry out Britney's final wish and built her orphanage in the coastal town of Grand Goave. The orphanage includes housing for thirty-three boys and thirty-three girls, a medical clinic, and earthquake-resistant walls. Shaped like the letter B, the Be Like Brit Orphanage is a lasting tribute to a young woman who dedicated herself to the wellbeing of others.

Even if the Gengels had built this orphanage in Boston, I'd be pretty impressed. After all, it's no easy feat to build a massive orphanage and fund it no matter where it is. But they built theirs in Haiti, right where Britney wanted it. Every tool, truck, and machine had to be sent by boat to this poor third-world country that doesn't even have postal service! But Haiti now has an earthquake-resistant orphanage thanks to a young woman REACH!ing out to help a nation in need, the REACH! she felt from its loving citizens, and the immeasurable REACH! that she and her parents have over all those who helped create this wonderful gift.

It's breathtaking to see the number of people who Len and Cherylann have influenced. They have created an army of people who would do anything—and I mean anything—for them. Is it easy to lose a daughter and decide to live out her last dream? Absolutely not. It's probably the hardest thing most of us could ever attempt. Pulling it off takes major REACH!—and creates so much more in the process. You can read about Britney Gengel and the Be Like Brit orphanage in the Gengels' book, *Heartache and Hope in Haiti*. I hope the book REACH!es you like it did me.

This chapter is all about cultivating your giving spirit and creating positive REACH! in your local and global community. But these aren't just things you should practice when you're off the clock. They come in very handy in your professional life as well.

People in need aren't the only ones who want help. We all want to be helped, whether we're recipients of charity or clients in a high-class store. We all have wants, needs, and desires; and the salesperson who caters best to them has the best shot of landing our business and expanding his or her REACH!. If you are in sales, stop trying to sell what *you have* and instead focus more on what your *customer wants*.

And don't forget to REACH! out to your own coworkers as well—whether you are an entry-level rookie or the CEO. Everyone has the power to create goodwill and positive REACH! within a company and everyone benefits from a more positive work environment, workers and clients alike. Is there someone you work with who could use some business mentoring? Don't wait for them to ask; just start. Perhaps there's someone within your company who appears to be stressed. REACH! out and extend a kind word or simply offer a shoulder to lean on.

If you are a company leader or owner, are you doing enough to REACH! back to help your people? Are you offering your people the ability to grow professionally and personally? Is there opportunity for your people to get coached? Is there someone within the company they can REACH! out to if they need emotional or financial support? If there's one thing that companies don't do enough, it's REACH! back to support their own employees. Most large companies have charitable committees and often times their own charitable foundations, and still too often forget to REACH! within.

Each holiday season, I make it a point to send an email to my entire company to see if anyone needs help providing a great holiday experience for their kids. To me, it just doesn't make sense to help outside organizations like The Salvation Army unless I first take care of those closest to me. There are always a handful of people in my firm who need the help just as much as those I am helping on the outside. If you are looking to create greater REACH! with your employees, make sure you don't forget to REACH! out to them too.

My friend and business partner Ann Marie is the best when it comes to REACH!ing out. She will REACH! out to tell you when you are doing something right. She will REACH! out to say hello if she hasn't heard from you in a while. She will even REACH! out to tell you when you are totally screwing up. She's like a guiding light in the lives of those around her. She has deep-seated values of right and wrong and she makes sure that not only is she sticking to them, but that everyone else is too. One of the best benefits of a true friendship is a friend's ability to REACH! back and help you stay on the path to your greatest dreams and ambitions—whether that means cheering you down the path or reminding you when you've stepped off it.

REACH! Challenge

1. REACH! out to one person every day and offer him or her a gift of your time, even if it's only five minutes. Volunteering for countless hours like Patti is great but not necessary. Just REACH! out once a day to offer someone your services, guidance, or your company. Before long you'll notice you will have created some truly powerful REACH! for yourself—and those around you.

2. Plan your own "Party with a Purpose!" Host a gathering at your home or office and have guests bring gifts for those in need. For example, collect canned goods for the local food pantry or collect clothing and toys for a local homeless shelter.

Visit www.REACHTools.net for free
downloadable REACH! resources.

Chapter 7
Techno-REACH!

"Social media is your opportunity to reach a massive number of people with transparency, honesty, and integrity." - Brian E. Boyd Sr.

Is REACH! easier to gain today than it was twenty years ago? Hell yeah, it is! With Facebook, Twitter, LinkedIn, and more than a dozen other social media networks, we have the ability to stay connected with millions and millions of people all the time. I now get to connect regularly with people I went to high school and college with, as well as complete strangers from all around the globe, day or night. And that's on top of the millions of strangers who have read my blog posts.

Let's talk Facebook for a minute. I write different types of content for the different blogs I work on. If an entry is business-related, it's usually on www.staceyalcorn.com, www.P3Coaching.com, or www. HuffingtonPost.com/Stacey-Alcorn. If it's fashion or REACH!-related, I post it on www.MyLittleBlackBox.com. The beauty of

Facebook is that I can target all of my blog content to my personal friends and/or fans of my businesses since each one has its own Facebook page. Even better, I can pay Facebook a few dollars to promote certain posts so that they show up on more followers' newsfeeds, resulting in even more traffic on my businesses' main websites.

Does any of that matter? I say yes. Social media enables me to REACH! more people with my message. I have the opportunity to REACH! literally millions more people online than I do in person alone by promoting my blog from the comfort of my modest little home in the suburbs of Boston. I get to REACH! out while I'm in my pjs! It's a really great feeling. If I wanted to achieve the same promotional exposure for my writing twenty years ago, I would have had to rent advertising space on a major network and develop a television commercial, much the same way author and visionary Tony Robbins got his start. Today, I have the ability to create major REACH! for pennies while sitting at home, at an airport, or anywhere else in the world that provides an Internet connection.

One key thing to understand about social media sites is that they're really impersonal. Creating REACH! through these channels isn't just about using them, but using them to learn more about people so that you can REACH! out to them in meaningful ways. Facebook, for instance, is not touchy-feely like an actual networking group where you go out and spend time with people *in person*. Wishing friends a happy birthday on their Facebook Walls is not nearly as nice as meeting someone for a birthday lunch or even just picking up the phone and calling them. Even if you get one hundred "Happy Birthday" wishes on Facebook, it's not the same as someone sending you a handwritten card. That being said, you can make Facebook feel more personal than most do, and create stronger bonds and greater REACH! in the process.

Here's how to do it: You probably spend 15 minutes a day on Facebook, posting photos, adding status updates, and browsing through other people's status updates to see what's going on in their lives. Next time, instead of simply commenting on one of their posts and leaving it at that, REACH! just a little, you can strengthen the bond you want to make or maintain, and turn an impersonal REACH!-out into a personal one.

When I'm scrolling through my Facebook feed each day and see that someone is having a bad day, I prescribe that person a book that I think will help. It's my way of saying, "I hear you! You are not alone! I want to help you." Upon seeing a friend post about a bad day on Facebook, you could do what most would do and write "Hope it gets better" on his or her Wall. It does acknowledges your friend's bad day, but will he or she likely remember your comment in one week? How about one year? Probably not. If however, you up your relationship ante by sending along a book or handwritten note to acknowledge your friend's suffering, you will have likely made a memorable impression that he or she will remember for weeks, maybe even years to come. Of course, this requires REACH!. However, when you REACH!, you create stronger REACH! within your network. People engage more on social media with those who have a more personal touch. More engagement means more meaningful relationships—and more of them as others start to notice their friends corresponding with you.

The Internet has also fundamentally changed how we promote and access a medium that goes back thousands of years: books. My last book, *Tuned In: Eight Lessons to Sales Success a Great Salesman Did Not Know He Knew,* was a self-published book. I have sold 10,000 copies since it was published, some through individual online sales and some through corporate purchases in conjunction with large speaking events. In the twentieth century, this was all but unheard of. Not only did most individual authors lack the networking and marketing capabilities to sell that many books on their own, but they also lacked the necessary funds. A self-published book was extremely expensive to produce as recently as the early 2000s. Today, both printing and distributing books are so inexpensive that many authors are choosing this route over working with traditional publishing houses.

Today, a relatively new author (like me) can sell thousands of books and even gain best-seller status without the assistance of a major publishing house. Self-published books are now commonplace on the virtual shelves of online stores like Amazon and Barnes & Noble. Most consumers do not care whether the books they are purchasing are published by authors or traditional publishers; they mainly just want to find well-written content on topics that matter to them. And thanks to social media, authors can market their self-published works very effectively. Sites like Facebook, Twitter, and blogs enable authors to introduce their work to audiences both broad and targeted that would have otherwise not heard about it. They can also easily track online sales since most online booksellers offer monthly reports that reveal when and where books are being bought.

If you were under the belief that publishing a book was out of your REACH! because you can't compete for a publisher, you were wrong. You don't even need one. Write your book, find a print distribution warehouse like Author House, Create Space, or Snowfall Press that will print on demand as orders are placed through Amazon.com or other online book retailers, get yourself an ISBN number (also quick and cheap to do), and start selling online. That's the power of having a global network literally at your fingertips.

REACH! is about going after what you want in life and also about creating a network of influence. Social media are powerful tools for achieving both. Think for a minute about the power of LinkedIn to maintain relationships and open doors to connections you never knew existed. If I wanted a particular job, I would start my search on LinkedIn. I would figure out who I know at the company I've been eyeing, for instance. Even if I knew no one, I'd still use LinkedIn to connect with people from that firm, and I would find out what organizations or networks they are involved in. Then I would join those networks—and probably even committees within those networks. Through the connections I could establish on this one site alone, I'm guessing I could probably have a job at that company within two weeks.

Through LinkedIn and its InMail, you have an email correspondence connection to almost anyone in the world you want. InMail costs $40-50 per month, but enables you to directly connect with hundreds of millions of users outside of your network. As I mentioned earlier: When you're REACH!ing, these are relatively small investments helping you get to a much larger end.

Recently I hosted an Extraordinary Women conference in Boston. I needed a keynote speaker and I knew whom I wanted. I wanted Bonnie Kirchner. She's an accomplished writer and speaker who teaches women who to trust with their money. Bonnie knows this subject all too well. In 2004, she found out her notorious now-ex-husband Brad Bleidt had embezzled $30 million from people in a Bernie Madoff-type pyramid scheme since the mid-1980s. Bonnie, had no idea her husband was doing this. But because Brad's name was on most of their marital assets, almost everything Bonnie owned was seized, including her home. She lost most of her assets and even her job as a financial expert on a major television network.

Not only did Bonnie live to tell her tale—she has told it to millions through the amazing investment advisory business she has built. She also penned an outstanding book, *Who Can You Trust With Your Money?*, which offers advice on choosing the right people to help you manage your investments, and ways to better protect yourself from scams. I wanted Bonnie at my event so bad I could taste it. How did I get her? Easy; LinkedIn. I REACH!ed out to her via InMail and asked her to come speak. She said yes! She offered insightful knowledge to our two hundred attendees and my own network has increased with the addition of this resilient woman who faced hard times and REACH!ed beyond them to make an amazing life for herself. Thanks to my REACH!ing out and Bonnie REACH!ing back, we created more REACH! for one another and further empowered everyone who attended the event.

Gary Vaynerchuk is an expert when it comes to creating REACH! on social networks. He built a $50 million empire in the wine business, and later grew a separate media business out of his wine company by using social media. Growing up, Gary worked in his father's liquor store and quickly got the idea to sell wine online. His father thought he was a little nuts, asking him, "Who would buy wine online?" As it turns out, lots of people. Gary initially attracted these potential buyers to his business by hosting an online wine show where he reviewed different wines in his unique, over-the-top fashion. (I've even heard him compare a wine to dirty socks.) He recorded daily episodes on a $400 FlipCam, and then eventually his iPad and iPhone. He then posted them on YouTube, Twitter, Facebook, and several other social media sites. The videos quickly went viral—and so did his business. Gary's videos were about reviewing the wine, not selling the product. However, by concentrating on offering value, hundreds of thousands of clients flocked to his online store to buy wine. Gary retired from making these videos in 2011 but you can still view them at www.DailyGrape.com.

But Gary didn't stop there. This master marketer was about to grow his online business tenfold. He did it by employing a tactic most business people do not: He started using social media as his *ears*, rather than his *mouth*.

Gary knew that the power of social media is in listening. While every business is sounding off about its great products or services it thinks you should buy, your clients and potential clients are talking all day long as well. All you have to do to listen is power up your computer or mobile device. Listen, *really* listen to what they are saying, and respond with a personal touch and perhaps some advice or other useful information. This is exactly what Gary Vaynerchuk did. If he noticed someone on Twitter looking for wine advice, he'd answer. Mind you, that person wasn't asking for *his* advice per se, but for *someone* in the Twitterverse to provide an answer. Gary would answer these people and create real and personal connections in the process—even though he was tweeting for his business. Traditional ads and mailings *cannot* start instant back-and-forth conversations between real people. But social media can. And Gary does, all the time.

What's truly powerful about these social media connections is that they REACH! more than just the person Gary's responding to. Thanks to the use of "hashtags" (keywords that start with a # sign), Twitter and Facebook conversations are public and searchable, meaning that anyone interested in topics you're discussing can find your posts—and in turn, you. It's like talking to one person in a room and having millions magically hear you at the same time. Gary made sure to insert himself into as many Twitter conversations about wine as he could. Before long, he was a recognized expert on wine across the site. As of the publishing of this book in fall 2013, Gary (@garyvee) has nearly one million followers.

I didn't use social media as an active listening tool until I read Gary's two *New York Times* bestsellers: *The Thank You Economy* and *Crush It.* Now I scroll through my newsfeeds daily and look for opportunities to cheer someone up, offer them helpful tips, or congratulate them. Last year, I noticed a real estate agent I was trying to recruit to my firm on Facebook posting photos of her dog's birthday cake. I sent the pooch a card and a small gift. And *boy*, was that real estate agent blown away. In this increasingly impersonal world we live in, you'll really catch people off guard when you pay attention to them—in a good way. Did I end up landing this agent at my company? No. But I have landed many other great agents at the firm by simply listening to them on social media and REACH!ing out to them in nontraditional ways. For example, two years ago I saw a post on Facebook that a real estate agent at another firm, Deb, was trying to help her son sell chocolate to raise money for his school. I emailed her through Facebook and offered to buy $100 worth of the chocolate since I knew the money was going to a good cause. That donation was the start of a wonderful friendship between Deb and I. She now works at my firm, and all because of the power of social media. The reason I wanted to share both stories here is to illustrate that you cannot look at this as an "if/then" relationship builder, as in: "If I send this real estate agent's pooch a card, she will come work for me." It doesn't work that way. This is about using social media to open doors, create relationships, and promote REACH!. The illusion of social media is that we think it's a great place to talk. But the business leaders who are "crushing it" like Gary Vaynerchuk recognize that *real* REACH! is achieved by listening first.

Twitter, Facebook, Tumblr, Pinterest, Instagram, Reddit, MySpace… they all create REACH! in different ways. They definitely create audience. And when you can establish an audience, then you have the ability to REACH! out and cultivate some real relationships with people you may not have otherwise had the ability to influence.

If you don't believe that social media can really create incredible influence, consider this: Many political experts have credited social media with helping Barack Obama win both his presidential elections. As of Election Night 2012, Obama had 32 million Facebook fans, 21 million Twitter followers, and 259,685 YouTube views. His main opponent, Mitt Romney, had just 12 million Facebook fans, 1.7 million Twitter followers, and only 29,172 YouTube views. It's difficult to say if social media was the principal reason why Obama won. But it is safe to say that a social media platform that enables you to REACH! at least 20 million more people than your main competitor gives you a very powerful advantage.

Since we are on the subject of creating great influence by building online social platforms, I feel like I have to spend a moment talking about one of my favorite websites for creating REACH!. It's called Help a Reporter Out (HARO); the website is www.helpareporter. com. This is a site where reporters, producers, writers, bloggers, you name it, REACH! out to people every day to ask for help creating their articles or shows. Most often, they are looking for experts to quote or interview. If you REACH! out to these folks regularly with content that helps complete or improve their stories, you can start some great relationships with powerful influencers and credential yourself and/or your business among both broad and targeted audiences. If ever there was a one-stop website for exponentially expanding your REACH!, this is it.

If you Google my name, you will find me quoted in hundreds of articles and blogs. Much of this is because of HARO. Monday through Friday, three times a day, HARO sends out its "Pitches," long lists of journalists looking for experts to talk to. I respond regularly to the ones I am interested in, the ones that really play to my strengths. Nearly once a week, journalists will contact me back, and I'll end up getting quoted in articles related to all sorts of industries. Plus, when I need to REACH! out to experts for my own articles and interviews, I often do it by posting a request on HARO. It gives me access to amazing experts from around the world who are passionate about the subject I am writing about. And trust me, if you post requests for expert opinions on HARO, somebody somewhere is bound to answer it. The people who answer HARO Pitches want the exposure just as badly as you want their expertise.

So, how do you know if you have REACH! when it comes to social media. Interestingly enough, there are several free programs that measure your influence including Klout, TwentyFeet, and Crowd Booster. The one I use for measuring influence is Klout (www.klout. com). Klout is a site that quantifies your influence relative to other users on a 1–100 scale (when this book was released in fall 2013, Barack Obama had the highest Klout score: 99).

Here's how you use Klout: You manually link to all of your social media sites: Facebook, Twitter, Google+, LinkedIn, Foursquare, Instagram, and more. Klout then measures your influence based on how many followers you have across these sites and how often users engage with your posts (commenting on, "Liking," or sharing/ retweeting them). As of June 2013, Klout reported that its average user's score was 40. Those with Klout scores of 63 or higher were in the top 5 percent.

You may be asking right now, "Who cares?" Well, apparently lots of businesses. They are starting to send special offers called Klout Perks to people with high Klout scores. These can range from dining coupons and movie sneak previews to exclusive trips. In 2013, Sony gave a group of influential outdoorsmen two new Sony cameras to try out—as part of a free coastline tour, aquarium trip, and paragliding adventure!

Why did Sony do that? Simple. It's good for business.

The people Sony invited on this trip have huge social influence among the target consumer group for Sony's new cameras. Anyone who had a great time would surely talk it up to their networks, creating genuine interest for these products among people who personally know and trust them. One participant called the trip "the most exhilarating thing" she's ever done. Talk about making social media more personal! In the same spirit, American Airlines knows that if it offers special Perks like free use of its high-end airport luxury lounges to people with high Klout scores, then those people will very likely share their great experiences on their social networks, in essence serving as organic, genuine spokespeople for a business they don't even work for.

For a low investment, great businesses are seeing the power of capitalizing on social Klout. If traditionally successful businesses are embracing the power of social media, you should too. It's a great way to stay within REACH! of your personal networks, REACH! out to expand those networks, and credential yourself and/or your business as a worthy and valuable player in your area of expertise.

And who knows... There may be some cool Klout Perks in it for you, too.

REACH! Challenge

1. Use your ears on Facebook today. Scroll through your Facebook newsfeed and find someone who you can REACH! out to—and I don't mean simply commenting on a Facebook update. I'm talking about picking up the phone, sending a card, or even sending a gift that acknowledges a post that a friend made on Facebook.

2. Sign up for www.HelpAReporter.com alerts to find out about unique opportunities to showcase your expertise in order to achieve even greater REACH!.

3. Pull out your list of REACH! goals from Chapter 2 and identify possible advocates among your LinkedIn contacts who can help you achieve them—or at least which of your contacts know other possible advocates. Once you identify these people, invite them out for a coffee or simply find out what networks they are involved in (usually listed on public LinkedIn profiles) and join them.

4. Sign up for Klout or other site that quantifies your social media influence to start monitoring your own social media influence and progress. Aim to one day be in the top 5 percent of users on that site (for example, achieve a Klout score in the sixties).

Visit www.REACHTools.net for free
downloadable REACH! resources.

Chapter 8

Smartphones, Tablets, and Apps... *Oh, My!*

"The important thing about mobile is: Everybody has a computer in their pocket. The implications of so many people connected to the Internet all the time from the standpoint of education is incredible." – Ben Horowitz

Now that we've covered some pretty powerful ways to REACH! for your dreams as well as ways to create REACH! for your life or business via social media tools, I wanted to spend a few moments talking about two other tech tools that have created a REACH! revolution: smartphones/tablets and apps.

Traditional telecommunications may sometimes create a hindrance to REACH!ing for your goals. With all that they offer in terms of communicating with others from afar, there is still no substitute for face-to-face contact. If you've ever REACH!ed for a better job or a new client, for example, you're more likely to establish rapport and trust with those you need to influence if you meet with them in person. But now with the advent of smartphones and tablets with video capabilities, you can meet people face to face no matter how far away you are from them.

First, here's a quick story about *why* it's so important to meet people face to face. In 2009, I was in the market for a car. Every day, I would drive past this one particular car lot on my ride to and from my office, and one day I spotted the car I wanted. I had test-driven cars of the same make and model in the past and loved it so there was no need to test-drive that one. I Googled the dealership and found all the info on the car I'd just seen, including the asking price and several interior and exterior photos. It was mid-spring and the photos all had snow in them, so I knew that I wouldn't have to pay full price for a vehicle that had sat on the lot for that long. I called the car dealership, asked for a salesperson, and offered him $3,000 below the asking price. What was his response? "Come on in and we can talk about pricing."

I should tell you: I hate dealing with salespeople. I know, you'd think I would have greater compassion for fellow salespeople. I coach people in the art of overcoming objections in my business, and the last thing I want to do in my spare time is volley back and forth offering objections to a salesperson who doesn't take no for an answer. As well, my biggest pet peeve with car salespeople is that they can really take up your time. I've actually been in a face-to-face car negotiation that took up half a day. Of course, this salesperson wanted to get in front of me. If you are in sales, you should always do your best to get in front of your clients. They can't fall in love with you on the Internet. When people fall in love with a business, they are loyal to it, and they spend more time and money on it. I didn't want to fall in love with this business; I just wanted that car at the best price. So I told the salesperson I was busy, had no interest in coming in, and was more than familiar with the vehicle so I did not intend to test-drive it.

The salesman declined my offer. A month went by and I kept driving past that car on the lot. I called again. I talked to the same salesperson and he tried to get me to come in. I would have no part of it. I made the same offer: $3,000 off the listed price. The salesperson countered at $1,500 off. I declined.

Another month went by, and I left the salesperson a message that I was still interested in the car, but only at my price. At the end of the summer, *four* months after I first saw the car, the salesperson called and said, "We will take your price." The next day I purchased the car.

If you are a salesperson, you are always going to get the short end of the stick if you can't see, hear, and shake the hand of your client. It is impossible to create rapport over email and nearly impossible to do it over the phone. Does that mean you are in trouble if your client base is in another state or country? Of course not. There *are* ways to create lasting, positive REACH! with strangers by phone; the key is seeing the person you are talking to. That's why the invention of products like smartphones and tablets, leveraged with programs like FaceTime and Skype, offer us a whole new way to communicate with the world. Now we can have face-to-face meetings with customers, friends, and family no matter the distance between the parties. And it's totally inexpensive—often free.

Back in 2000, a face-to-face meeting across oceans would have cost hundreds of dollars per hour, and the audiovisual quality was often less than desirable. I remember participating in such satellite meetings and hearing an odd voice delay where you could see the person talking on the screen but it would take a few seconds for the sound to catch up. Today face-to-face conferencing is so easy that my three-year-old can do it—and she often does, using FaceTime to communicate with me when I'm travelling the country. The audiovisual quality is great too. It's like having my daughter sitting with me at breakfast even when we are four thousand miles apart. What would have happened if my car salesman had FaceTimed me? Could he have developed rapport with me? Probably more than he created through voicemails and phone conversations.

With smartphones and tablets, we also see many great social apps being developed that allow for greater REACH!. Foursquare is a fun app with which people "check in" at their favorite businesses to announce to the world where they are. My greatest immediate benefit to using Foursquare is that I can see where my connections are hanging out regularly and decide to visit there myself to create more opportunities for in-person networking. Plus as a business owner, I can REACH! out to regular customers and increase their sense of loyalty by offering them specials and incentives just for checking in. Much like Klout Perks, these exclusive offers reward my clients for their online engagement and, in the process, forge greater personal relationships.

Another app I use often is Yelp. In days of old (pre-2004), we had to risk trying out a restaurant all on our own to see if it had good food and service. Sure, we could ask friends or coworkers if they'd been there before, but that only worked with some local establishments. Today with Yelp at my fingertips, I can find the best restaurants around me in seconds, as reviewed by millions of people I've never met and would never think to ask. Yelp is a social app powered by consumers who rate and review restaurants along with other businesses and service providers. New to your area? Yelp can help you find a great dentist, dry cleaner, or real estate agent. Visiting a new vacation spot? Yelp knows the best shoe repair spot within walking distance to your hotel. Plus, since the advent of Yelp (and social media in general), businesses have felt more accountable to their customers, which ideally encourages them to create a better customer experience—or pay the penalty in the form of a bad review gone viral.

Like all the other social tools we've discussed, Yelp is a tech tool that can help create positive REACH! in the real world for customers and businesses alike.

Now that we've covered some great ways to develop in-person rapport through your phone, it's time to be more face-to-face with your emails.

Send more effective emails to your clients, friends, and family with apps like Eyejot, Mailbox, or Talk Fusion. Instead of typing, you record a video message on your desktop, laptop, tablet, or phone that you then send to your receiving party's email. When they click "Play," they can see and hear what you have to say, rather than try and understand your tone through impersonal, emotionless text. It's like putting your email on steroids.

And we're not even limited to sending videos of our email messages. Thanks to digital cameras being embedded into our tablets and smartphones, we now have the ability to take photos and videos, and text or email them anywhere in the world.

Nothing says you're having fun in New York City like a text or email of a picture of you atop the Empire State Building or a video of you dancing next to the Naked Cowboy in Times Square. In fact, thanks to apps like Over, you can write captions right onto your pictures before you send them. Or by using Instagram, you can apply different lighting filters to your pictures or videos and instantly share them with friends across *all* of your social media platforms at once.

I haven't been this excited about sharing photos since I was 12 years old.

I had a Polaroid Instamatic camera and I loved it! Instead of waiting days for older film to develop after taking a photograph, I could finally have a fully developed photo in *minutes* to share with people sitting right in the room with me. Today, we have thousands of apps at our fingertips that help us share sights, sounds, and real emotions in real time with millions of people around the world. Now that's REACH!.

How do you find good apps that make life and business easier? One way is to ask others in your network what they are using. It is my experience that people love to share their good app experiences. You can find books and magazines dedicated to sharing the best apps for Android phones, iPhones, and iPads in any local or online bookstore. If you are looking for a fun way to share apps, try an "appy hour" where you invite a group together for lunch or cocktails with the specific goal of sharing your favorite apps. There are more than one million apps in the Apple iStore alone, so choosing the right ones for you is important. "Quality over quantity" is the key to creating REACH! most effectively when using this type of media. Seek out the best ways to narrow your search and find apps that will quickly create the REACH! you are looking for.

If you think it's too late to try these tools yourself, guess what? It's not. We're all experimenting on these platforms every day to see what works and what doesn't. Those who spend more time experimenting will create more REACH! for themselves. It's as simple as that.

For you business owners out there, these technology tools are a great way to build your employee, contractor, and vendor networks as well. Twenty years ago, my selection for employees, contractors, and vendors was limited to a 100-mile radius around my office. Today, I can forge close relationships with vendors worldwide thanks to sites like Elance.com and Freelancer.com. My web designer, Bhupendra, works in India. My virtual assistants live in Oklahoma and Illinois. My graphic designer resides in Canada. www.elance.com and www.

freelancer.com both have protections built in to make sure your work gets done on time and for the price you and your vendors agree to.

So now we know how to be more immediate, personal, and far-reaching with our phone calls, emails, and photo/video sharing. But writing, calling, and taking pictures are things we've all been able to do for a long time—we're just better at them now. But what about media we haven't always been able to take part in? Modern technology helps us access those too.

Take radio for instance. Twenty years ago, it was virtually impossible to start your own radio show. We the People were mostly consumers of radio, not active participants. You needed to be extremely well connected, and also it helped if you had money behind you.

Today that's simply not the case. There are sites like Blogtalk Radio and Contact Talk Radio that, for a small fee, enable you to share your ideas and content with the world via live radio feeds. My friend Marilee Driscoll runs an extremely popular radio talk show broadcasted nationwide through Contact Talk Radio. Her show, 9 Hour Reset (www.9HourReset.com) reaches thousands, allowing her a platform to further build her marketing, coaching, and consulting business. What's even more exciting is that she has monetized her radio program by selling ad spots as well as paid co-host spots. Now the world gets to hear from a renowned expert like Marilee Driscoll, without the millions of dollars and a pocket full of industry connections once required.

Even on-camera notoriety can be obtained by anyone outside of the television and movie industries now, thanks to YouTube. It's expensive and usually cost prohibitive to buy TV programming. But why go there when most of your viewing audience is equally accessible online. Consider these facts:

- Over four billion videos are viewed each day on YouTube.

- Over 800 million unique users visit YouTube each month.

- Over three billion hours of video are watched each month on YouTube.

- More video is uploaded to YouTube in one month than three major U.S. networks created in 60 years.

- YouTube is accessible in thirty-nine countries and fifty-four languages.

- In 2011, YouTube had more than one trillion views.

- In 2011, there were almost one hundred forty views for every person on earth.

With YouTube, you can create your own movie or episode series and share it with the world. Some entrepreneurs are even monetizing YouTube by selling their brands and services through their videos. And others have become so popular among viewers (and therefore advertisers) that they earn money just by posting new content and garnering millions of views. Just like the radio, you don't need big money and connections to get your brand noticed.

These sites are great for business and personal REACH! alike. According to a 2011 report by MarketData Enterprises, 30 percent of college students are taking their classes online. According to a 2013 study by StatisticBrain.com, more than forty million people have tried online dating. When it comes to finding love or a higher degree, you are no longer confined to your own geographic network. The possibilities for what you can bring into your life through technology are endless. All you have to do is embrace them.

REACH! Challenge

1. Organize an "appy hour" at your office so you and your coworkers have the ability to share your favorite apps.

2. Have you had an itch to learn something specific for a long time? It could be as involved earning a Bachelor's degree or as simple as learning how to blog, knit, or run long distances. Whatever it is, research it online. There's a good chance that you will find a YouTube video or other online learning platform that will offer you the instruction you need to REACH!.

3. Pull out your REACH! goals and identify which technology tools in this chapter can help you move closer to your goals.

Visit www.REACHTools.net for free
downloadable REACH! resources.

Chapter 9

Delegation

"Surround yourself with the best people you can find, delegate authority, and don't interfere as long as the policy you have decided upon is being carried out." – Ronald Reagan

Delegation has been one of the most difficult things for me to learn. It is the process by which you give up control of some of your daily tasks so that someone else can do them for you. That's right, it's all about getting an assistant, handyman, housekeeper, or anyone to help you accomplish what you need to accomplish each day. It's not easy for some of us to relinquish this type of control. But if you learn how, your reward will be loads of positive REACH!.

We all have a highest and best use of our time, meaning something that we really enjoy doing or something that we get paid well to do—preferably it's both. Everyone's highest and best use of time is different, but the lesson for us all is the same: Any work that you do on a daily basis that you don't like doing or that you don't get paid well to do should be done by someone else, period. The theory behind this is that if you pay someone to do your low-value tasks, it gives you more time to focus on your high-value ones.

I mentioned earlier that while I was working my way through college, I started flipping houses. Most of these houses needed lots of reconstruction work, known as "rehab," before I could sell them. I cannot swing a hammer, and I have no interest in swinging a brush—or doing any handy work for that matter. I don't like it. Roughly twenty of my properties ended up needing rehab, and I hired people to do the dirty work every time.

Eventually, my parents caught my rehab bug and they started buying and selling properties, too. The problem is that my dad is really handy so he started spending more time sanding the floors, painting, and building cabinets to rehab his properties—and *less* time growing and running his automotive shop. He didn't think the cost of doing his own rehab work was far more expensive than the cost of hiring a contractor to do it. But looking from the outside in, I could see that his rehabs were costing him way too much money *and time* to fix up, thereby depleting his profits. This was exacerbated by the fact that he was doing the work alone while a contractor would often bring in an entire crew. For every hour he could be making $60 running his automotive shop and paying a contractor $20 to sand his houses' floors, he was losing $40 by sanding the floors himself. This was a disaster—and my father couldn't see it. It wasn't until his auto business really slowed down that he realized he'd made a mistake by spending all his time on rehab properties. My dad eventually retired from flipping properties as his real passion is in rehabbing vehicles, not homes.

My father is not the only one who does this. Many of us have the same issue; it's just harder to see it when it's *your* issue. I joke with my fiancée and say that the reason we need a cleaning person two hours a week is that it's far less expensive for her to do the cleaning than it is for me to do it. I joke, but I'm also totally serious. If I worked those extra two hours, I would earn more than what it would cost to pay someone to clean my house in the meantime. And if I instead chose to spend those extra two hours with my daughter (as I often do), that activity would be more important to me than the money it costs to hire a cleaner *and* the time spent working. It's a win-win. By the way, if a professional cleaner is outside of your budget, what about a high school student in your neighborhood who would be willing to help around the house occasionally for a small stipend, better yet, why not your own kids?

Delegation is an important part of your REACH!. You can only REACH! so far by yourself; but with the help of others, you can REACH! way beyond yourself. A great visual demonstration of this concept is the 1986 fundraiser, Hands Across America. On the afternoon of Sunday, May 25, 1986, nearly seven million people held hands in a human chain for fifteen minutes that stretched across the continental United States. Those who wished to participate donated $10 to fight poverty. The chain was 4,152 miles long and stretched from New York City's Battery Park all the way to the RMS Queen Mary pier in Long Beach, California. No one person could ever reach from New York to California alone. But with the help of others, a 4,100-mile REACH! is possible. The organizers of that fundraiser had to REACH! out to inspire and coordinate the work of millions to achieve their goal. And so can you. You are absolutely, positively, without a doubt going to need help to achieve your greatest dreams and ambitions. That's just a fact. You need to magnify the power of you. How do you create two yous? You get help. Even if that person is not a duplicate of you, isn't 1.5 yous better than one? Get help!

My assistant enables me to get much more completed every day than if I were trying to complete all my tasks alone. It is because of her that I can attend networking lunches instead of returning emails and sit on charitable committees instead of always updating my social media feeds. Instead of having to go out and look at commercial space for new office locations, my assistant previews the choices and prepares an organized report that I can briefly review. She sends my thank you notes, helps me pay bills, and makes sure that I respond to missed calls. Before hiring an assistant, I did it all. She is so good that I'm now considering hiring a *second* assistant to further leverage my time and productivity. The highest and best use of my time is networking, speaking to large audiences, writing content, marketing, and generating new business leads. These are the tasks that I strive to do daily while my assistant takes care of my daily lower-value tasks.

Take out a pen and make a list of just ten things you do daily that are not the best use of your time. Cleaning, sorting mail, checking email, updating social networks, returning calls, paying bills, organizing your desk, sending thank you notes, booking appointments, etc. If you concentrate hard enough, you'll find plenty of low-value tasks in your life that others could do for you, saving you time and money. Your goal should be to create two yous, then three yous, then four.... Keep leveraging the power of "you" until you REACH! the highest and best use of your time—doing the things you love and/or make good money to do, and no longer wasting time or money on lower-value tasks.

Again, it's been difficult for me to learn how to let go of these tasks, delegate them to others, and spend more time REACH!ing. But I'm doing it by following these nine simple tips:

1. **Know Your Value**

Do you know how valuable you are? Do you know what your time is worth? Many of us don't. In fact, self-employed and commissioned salespeople—those who should be most concerned with making the most of their time—tend to be the worst delegators. They have an entire day in which to control their actions, as opposed to pay-rate employees.

So let's try to figure out what your time is worth—and what it could be worth when you start delegating more. For argument sake, let's say you made $50,000 last year. That's roughly $25 an hour. Now, write down three essential tasks that you performed daily to help bring in that $50,000 (e.g., prospecting calls, networking functions, generating referrals). Now, take a guess as to how much of your daily schedule is spent on these three tasks. If you say 50 percent, you are being very generous, but we will go with it. Assuming you work forty hours a week, this means that twenty of those hours are spent making the $50,000 and the other twenty are spent doing lower-value tasks like paperwork, returning calls, checking emails, driving around, and other non-essential work that does not directly impact your pay scale.

If you choose to delegate all the low-value, non-essential tasks you identified above and spent 40 hours a week doing the top three essential tasks that generate your income, you could stand to *double* your income. Every hour that you choose not to delegate a non-essential task, you are costing yourself up to $25. Yet you squawk at the notion of paying someone $15 per hour to do it for you. Why is that?

For many of us control freaks, we have to understand that a $15-per-hour personal assistant should not be expected to immediately generate $50,000 of income on their own. Generating the extra $50,000 is dependent on *you* maximizing the highest and best of *your* newly freed up work hours. Time and again I have witnessed really good salespeople hire talented assistants only to get rid of them six months later because they haven't seen an increase in their earnings. Most often, it's because he or she does not realize that the real advantage of having a personal assistant is that you, the boss, now have more hours to invest in your three moneymaking tasks. If your goal in hiring an assistant is to make more money, but you take longer to complete your moneymaking tasks (or use them solely to enjoy leisure activities), then you should curse yourself for coming up short, not your assistant. Income generation is and should always be your job and only your job. Everything else should get delegated to someone else.

Awesome delegators know the value of their time. That way they can easily calculate the return on value when they delegate any task, project, or commitment that would otherwise threaten to waste it.

2. **Baby Steps**

Creating lasting results often requires baby steps. I have traveled much of the United States and Canada coaching sales teams on how to increase sales, both consumers and other businesses. My number one piece of advice is to pick a really small number of calls you are willing to make each day and make them. The business owners who leave my event and begin a campaign of calling one hundred people a day for two weeks end up failing because there's no way they can sustain that type of activity and eventually abandon it. Those business owners, however, who leave my event and take baby steps, such as making five sales calls a day, often end up reaching their goals. Five calls a day is easy to accomplish. That's something most people can do on their ride to work.

If you are a mighty control freak like me, and delegating part of your day to others seems like an insurmountable challenge, then start really small. Pick one small piece of your day that you would be willing to delegate to someone else. Let's start simple with your weekend errands. Perhaps it's something as slight as opening and sorting the mail at your office. Hire someone to take care of this one small task. By taking baby steps, you begin to get a sense of the power you have over controlling your entire day.

What should you do with your time now that you've delegated the opening and sorting of mail? You have a few choices. First, you may choose to profit on your time by using it to earn money. Second, you might choose to relax or do something else you would rather do besides opening and sorting mail like reading a good book or going to the beach. This is fine, too. The point of working so hard during the week is so that you can enjoy your time off. You shouldn't feel like your nights and weekends are like a part-time job. By resting or enjoying something you love to do, you come back to work on Monday rejuvenated and ready to give your work your all. This will quite likely translate into higher profitability, especially if you are in a commissioned job. Third, you may end up using your additional time to tackle another project that's on your list, like painting the shed. Taking tiny steps in delegating your work and home chores will result in greater REACH!.

3. Delegation Partner

One of the best delegators I know is my business partner at P3 Coaching & Training, Jeff Wright. Jeff has a huge team of people that he delegates to, which has enabled him to grow and sustain multiple businesses simultaneously. He owns five large real estate offices in Connecticut, is one of the top three commercial real estate agents in the world within his real estate franchise, and constantly travels the world for speaking engagements. Without a doubt, he could not accomplish all of these things at the same time without an amazing team behind him managing daily operational tasks while he focuses on expanding his REACH! and that of his companies.

Over the years, Jeff has been a great delegation partner for me. In other words, when he sees that I am working on low-value tasks, he is quick to remind me that I need to delegate those tasks to someone else. It is because of Jeff that I finally broke down and hired a full-time personal assistant. Constantly, Jeff reminds me that if I focus solely on the few parts of my job that propel me toward my vision, I will get there a heck of a lot faster.

Find someone in your personal or professional life who understands the power of delegation and equally understands the highest and best use of *your* time. Invite this person to tell you when you're taking on too many low-value tasks and to encourage you to delegate them. Make sure to choose someone who has no problem calling you out when he or she catches you poorly prioritizing your day.

4. **Hire Slow, Fire Fast**

When it comes to trusting someone with your time and your REACH!, take your time hiring them.

I've learned my lesson when it comes to hiring people who do little for you in return. If you have had one or more bad experiences hiring people to help increase your productivity, just know that the right assistant is out there somewhere. Often times you won't land one of the great ones on the first try, but they're out there. One helpful tool I use when hiring assistants is a DISC profile tool. A DISC profile helps you assess four main personality traits in a candidate:

- DOMINANCE: How s/he shapes his/her environment by overcoming opposition to accomplish results;

- INFLUENCE: How s/he shapes the environment by influencing or persuading others;

- **STEADINESS:** How s/he cooperates with others within existing circumstances to carry out tasks; and

- **CONSCIENTIOUSNESS:** How s/he works conscientiously within existing circumstances to ensure quality and accuracy.

Conducting these assessments is free and easy. Simply register for a free DISC tool online (I use the one at www.TonyRobbins.com), send potential employees to the site to take the DISC questionnaire, and have them send the results back to you. A large percentage of applicants will not complete the task, potentially disqualifying them from the job by demonstrating their lack of ability to follow directions.

When an applicant sends the report back to you, read it thoroughly. You will have two booklets full of information about the type of person this candidate is. (The candidate also receives a complete rundown of his or her characteristics, along with the types of jobs s/he would most likely excel at.) Certain personalities work well with specific types of jobs. Some people are extremely social and outgoing, making them great influencers for a sales position, but they might lack attention to detail, which would make them poor candidates for a job in accounting. What kind of traits would your perfect assistant have? Match those traits with those outlined in your candidates' DISC profiles and you will be more likely to hire a perfect match.

Whether you employ the DISC profiling method or not, take your time in hiring someone whom you feel is a great fit for you. If your gut says "no," don't hire that person. Also if you hire someone and it doesn't work out in the first few weeks, don't stick it out. In just a couple of weeks, you will find out if this person has ambition, is timely, cares about the job, and is grateful for the opportunity to work for you. If it's not working out, just say so and move on. There are millions of candidates out there who would pine for the opportunity to work with you, so give someone else a chance—for their sake and yours.

5. **Empower Your Team**

Once you've made a solid hire, be sure to value and empower that person. Because when they succeed on their own, your team is far more likely to succeed as a team, and you are more likely to rake in larger profits. Plus, when the time comes for your talented employees to head off to more exciting jobs elsewhere, you will further expand your own REACH! by having contacts at other companies that trust and respect you and your company.

If there is one damaging mistake I see leaders often make, it is that they undervalue their teams. They do not realize the precious gems that sit before them. Even worse, when their team members rise to the occasion, these misguided leaders will try their hardest to stomp them back down for fear that they will fly off and accomplish their dreams somewhere else.

I want my assistant to learn countless lessons from working with me. I hope that I help empower her to do great things. I want to hear her voice when she has ideas about new and better ways to grow my business and I want the world to hear it too. I encourage her to take on new tasks that she enjoys as she discovers her own highest and best use of her time. I insist that she maintain a blog about her work, life, and even random thoughts because I want her to know that she is powerful, amazing, and unstoppable.

Will I get to keep my assistant forever? I doubt it. I have had assistants who last for years and others who only stick around a few months. I know that my current assistant will one day want more than I can offer her; but until then, I want her to feel that her potential is limitless in my employ. I make sure she knows that as much as she is on my team, I am on hers too, and that I want to offer her my insights on how to achieve.

Loosen the Reins

U.S. Army General George S. Patton once said, "Don't tell people how to do things. Tell them what to do and they will surprise you with their ingenuity." I believe that great managers practice this principle every day. Most people don't work for money. Sure they want to be paid fairly, but most want other things out of a job like the ability to make a difference in an organization, lead projects, try out new ideas, and control their own schedules. Daniel H. Pink's book, *Drive: The Surprising Truth about What Motivates Us*, offers some awesome insights into what your people want. After reading his book, I reevaluated the way I work with my own team members and tried a new way of managing my assistant.

Now I have no set schedule for her; she can choose when and where she wants to work each day. She can work at any of our fourteen offices, at Starbucks, at home, or wherever she feels most productive. I don't need to know when she's leaving early or if she's taking a day off. All I want to know is that the jobs I've hired her to do get done. I am happy to report it's working brilliantly: She is the first assistant who has totally come through for me. Perhaps it is because I instituted a stronger hiring process by DISC profiling her. Maybe it's because she is just generally a driven, hard-working individual. And maybe, just maybe, it's because I not only loosened the reins on my assistant for the first time in my life, I let go of them all together.

You want every member of your team to be empowered to dream, stretch, achieve and influence because the more they REACH!, the stronger your team becomes. If you are constantly trying to rein your team members in, they will eventually just stop REACH!ing. They will come to work and do the minimum required of their job.

6. **Close Your Eyes and Let Go**

This is the part where you let the rubber hit the road. You've tried out the DISC profiling technique to find a great candidate for your job openings. Then you've made the decision to empower your employees and loosen the reins on them, giving them leeway to imagine new ways you can grow your business while leveraging your time. You are giving them the power to flourish. Now, it's time to give them work.

You have to let go of something.

Remember those non-essential tasks we talked about—the busywork, paperwork, returning emails, checking messages, etc.? Now it's time to delegate those tasks to your team. Make sure your assistants feel totally comfortable asking you questions along the way. If they perceive they are bothering you, they may try to answer a question themselves when they should really be asking for advice. Let them know you are available for any and all questions, and then pass along work to them.

It bears repeating here that your assistant is only as effective as what you do with your additional time. If you spend your newly freed up time reading books, going to movies, and golfing, you may end up finding that your assistant is an unnecessary expense. Always remember that delegation has two parts. The first is making sure that your team members are doing the work the way you want it to be done while also allowing them to try out new and better ways to do so. The second is learning how to concentrate on only those items that constitute the highest and best use of your time. You will know that you have found a groove with your team members when you start feeling confident handing over more difficult tasks to them. I recommend giving team members a full array of work to do right at the beginning so that you can get an idea of where they excel and where they need help. Some things will come naturally to your team while others will require a little training and oversight. Let them take on the former items with gusto while easing them into job duties that require more hand holding.

7. **Accountability**

Great delegators offer clear and manageable goals to their teams. How can your team possibly know if it is on course if it has no compass? It's imperative that we as leaders point our employees in the right direction and give them clear, concise, attainable goals to strive for every day. Here's a few examples of what I am talking about:

> VAGUE:
> I need you to check my email daily and tell me if there's anything important.
>
> CLEAR, CONCISE, ATTAINABLE:
> Please check my email once every hour throughout the day. If you see an email that is from a new client, a team member, or appears time sensitive, please call or text me immediately. If the email is an advertisement or marketing propaganda, please delete it.
>
> VAGUE:
> Check my voicemail regularly.
>
> CLEAR, CONCISE, ATTAINABLE:
> Check my voicemail once every hour throughout the day. Here is a list of potential calls that I would need to know about immediately.
>
> VAGUE:
> If you run out of work to do, organize the office.

CLEAR, CONCISE, ATTAINABLE:
If you run out of work to do, I've created a three-page checklist of weekly administrative items that need attention:

- Organize files

- Update the customer database

- Send out postcards

- Clean the office

- Check in with clients from the past ninety days to see how they are enjoying their products/services

Your overall delegation goal should be that your team members always know when they are winning, whether or not you tell them. For example, your assistant will know he is winning if you tell him to check your email once per hour and flag certain ones for you—and he does it. Or your marketing coordinator will know she is winning if you ask her to send out fifteen client emails a day and she completes the task. When you offer vague goals, you often get vague results. So be clear and leave little room for error.

When you are clear about your personal goals, it is much easier for your team to buy in to them and help you achieve them. Also let your team members take part in the celebration when you reach financial milestones, land large clients, etc. You want them to feel like each of your accomplishments is truly a team accomplishment, due in large part to the individuals who all contribute their share to create the win. Make them feel like winners and they will want to create more wins for you.

8. Feedback

Once you've outlined your expectations for what jobs need to get done and how, it's important to provide recognition for jobs done well and constructive feedback on how things can be improved. If you don't get feedback from your team members, you cannot expect them to become better than they already are. Here are some great questions to ask your team members regularly:

- On a scale of 1–10, with 10 being the best, how satisfied are you with your job?

- What could I do to bring your answer to a 10?

- What are your top three favorite aspects of your job?

- If you could have two additional key roles or tasks, what would they be?

- Where do you see yourself in three years?

- What are you doing daily in your job to get where you want to be three years from now?

- What's the greatest lesson you have learned here in the past thirty days?

Leaders who spend time REACH!ing back to those working for them end up creating more solid teams because by asking, they know what each team member needs in order to further grow into their positions. Remember the original goal of delegating? It's to create two, three, or even one hundred yous! If you want to effectively duplicate the role you have within your business, you need to find dependable team members, delegate to them, and then shift around their positions so that everyone is in the best position possible to help you maximize your overall productivity and profit. This is when you create maximum impact on your business and effectively leverage your time. You find out by asking them. And the more questions the better, since some may otherwise be reluctant to come out and tell you exactly what they like or don't like. But if you can earn your employees' trust and ask them genuine questions about ways to improve their work experience, the truth will come out.

Feedback, however, must go both ways.

Creating positive REACH! among your employees requires that you praise them when they are doing well and let them know when they are falling behind or not meeting expectations. Those two things—along with clear, initial guidance on the jobs you'd like done and how—will help motivate your team to achieve great things. A great rule of thumb for providing constructive feedback in a way that maintains your employees' motivation is: Offer three positive pieces of feedback for every one negative. This way your team members know how much you appreciate them and that the small course corrections you offer do not reflect upon the overall value they offer to your team.

If your schedule is crazy like mine, it's easy to get so busy that you simply don't offer feedback, and the price you pay is mediocre results. "Their work is good enough," you might say in order to avoid the painful job of facing the people who need constructive feedback.

I've seen busy leaders take this route too many times, and often it ends badly. Mediocre performance compounds over time in the form of accrued productivity and revenue lost. It may eventually get to the point where you end up firing an employee who very well could have been great with just a little bit of direction. Then you lose a potentially valuable employee *plus* the time it will take to recruit and train a replacement.

If you have an assistant, the ideal would be that he or she enables you to duplicate your performance and income by concentrating on your top three essential tasks. He or she may very well have the potential to create two yous, but you are settling for 1.25 yous if you do not offer constructive feedback on areas that can be improved and praise for jobs well done. This directly impacts your day and your paycheck.

Again, be sure your team gets plenty of initial guidance, feedback, and praise—the three most important things you can provide in order to help them REACH! their highest productivity possible.

9. It's Not a Business Thing; It's a Life Thing

I have spent a large portion of this chapter talking about the importance of delegating to a *work* team. Done properly, it will positively impact your income, your assets, and your ability to REACH!. That being said, the most important people I delegate to daily are people outside of work. I have a house cleaner, a babysitter, a handyman, a contract courier, and sometimes a personal driver. (I'll hire one for long road trips because I know the work I do while in that car will offset the expense.) These people create wins for me and enable me to focus on all my high-value tasks, both personal and professional. For that reason, they require and deserve the same clear direction, feedback, and positive reinforcement that my office employees do. Everyone you delegate to, everyone who helps you achieve more REACH!, needs these things no matter what time of day or physical setting you interact with them in.

Delegation is not always easy, but it's the right thing to do—for you *and* your employees. Never think of it as an expense, but rather as an investment into more time and/or money for you. Delegation is just another worthwhile—no, *critical*—investment into maximizing your REACH!.

REACH! Challenge

1. For the next seven days, keep a journal of what you are working on each hour throughout the day. You should include all tasks, both work and play.

2. Once you have a complete seven day list of tasks, go through and circle the essential tasks—the ones that are the highest and best use of your time; the tasks that cannot be delegated.

3. Of the items that should be delegated, try delegating five of those tasks to someone else. You can delegate to paid employees, contract workers, and even family—let your kids bring the trash out!

4. Once you've started delegating at least five tasks, keep a journal for another seven days. Note what you are doing while others are doing tasks you used to perform. Are you focusing on "highest and best use" tasks? If so, you have saved yourself time and or money by delegating. If, however, you continue to work on other low-value tasks, consider how to delegate those as well.

5. Monitor your progress weekly.

Visit www.REACHTools.net for free
downloadable REACH! resources.

Chapter 10

Stilettos and REACH!

"I have multiple personality disorder—in a very good way, of course—when it comes to my fashion choices." – Katy Perry

I love shoes. I have so many shoes that it's embarrassing to talk about. But I have to talk about it a bit here because, after all, my leopard skin six-inch stilettos with red souls definitely enhance my ability to REACH!.

I'll explain.

By now you know that I was an awful student, at least in high school. I didn't like going to class. Often times, my friends and I would cut school, rent movies, and go to someone's house to hang out all day. Back then we had what we called video stores. (It's funny that my three-year-old daughter will probably never understand the concept of a video store. But anyway...) I would get so frustrated at the local Blockbuster because I am exactly five feet tall and the New Release videos were always on the top shelf, which was just above my REACH!. Back then, I didn't understand how to REACH! higher for what I really wanted, so I always settled for the older videos that I could reach (lowercase). If I just understood the power of REACH!—or at least the value of a pair of shoes—those New Release movies would be all mine. My six inch leopard skin stilettos would have made all the difference in the world in getting what I wanted back then. So it is true today.

"Wait a minute," you might ask. "Why didn't you just ask for help if you couldn't reach the movie you wanted?" It comes down to self-assurance. I am not saying that every girl needs or even has to like a nice pair of stilettos like I do. However, I am suggesting that as you grow into your own sense of fashion or other style, it helps you develop assuredness. For me, a nice pair of shoes makes me feel like I can accomplish anything. Back then, I lacked the confidence to ask for help and to REACH! for what I wanted. Today I know I am capable of REACH!ing for anything. And for me at least, a little piece of that attitude comes along with a tailored suit and nice pair of shoes.

As I've mentioned earlier (and it bears repeating): *Confidence* is essential when you dream big with the intentions of stretching for and attaining your goal. I didn't always have confidence growing up. This is mostly because I was a short and chubby kid who didn't have much style. Back in my college days, when I was making copies at that mortgage company, my boss Mary Mitchell gave me some amazing advice that has stuck with me to this day.

See, I never dressed nice back then because I was just a copy machine girl. I wore jeans to work because nobody told me I couldn't. I didn't care what I looked like. Dressing nice seemed pointless to me because I rarely worked with customers as I was resigned to the copy machine all day. My boss, however, always looked like a million bucks—and to me, she looked like a millionaire. She always wore nice suits and beautiful shoes—she just radiated money from her pores. Whenever she came to the office, the employees, the customers, and even the mailman would comment on how good she looked. One day I complimented her on her suit, which included an eye-catching pink and orange plaid skirt. I will always remember what Mary replied with, and I hope you do, too: "Dress for the job you want," she said, "not the job you have."

Mary wasn't talking about her wardrobe; she was talking about mine, and I knew it right then. It was almost as if she had been waiting for an opportunity to tell me that I should dress better even though I had the lowest possible job you could have at that firm. She did me a huge favor by REACH!ing out to me that day and saying what she did. Looking back, it's definitely one of those key moments that changed my whole life's trajectory.

The following week, I came to work in a whole new wardrobe. I thought about the job I wanted and I dressed for it. My coworkers noticed the change immediately and they encouraged me by taking the time to comment on my new look. I was so encouraged in fact that I eventually tried out new colors and styles for my hair too. Oh, and by the way, I had to wear these nice suits to school as well, since I didn't have time to change after class. And you know what I gained at school? Respect. My teachers treated me differently and so did the other students. And we all know what you gain when people start noticing and respecting you more: Confidence.

Dressing for the job I wanted rather than the job I currently had forced to me to really consider where I wanted to go in my life and in my career. As I considered the direction of my life, I instinctively started taking steps toward realizing what it is I wanted. I was becoming bolder. My boss and coworkers were noticing me more and began treating me like more than a copy girl by giving me small opportunities to try out new things, leading me to ask for a job processing mortgages—which I got—and eventually into buying and selling real estate as an investor.

When I started flipping real estate, my confidence and my wardrobe played huge roles in my success. I was a twenty-year-old kid buying homes. Do you think contractors would have really taken me seriously if I showed up in jeans and a tank top? No way. But since I never dressed, walked, and talked like a kid, they never judged me like one. I showed up in a nice suit and high heels and they took me seriously.

Today, I dress up for work every day. I rarely wear jeans to work because I feel most confident and ready to REACH! when I'm wearing work clothes and nice shoes. I want people to respect me because it helps me maintain my confidence. In fact, I often dress professionally wherever I go (unless I'm out on a leisure activity). The reason is: I never know when or where I will meet the next person whom I need to REACH! out to. It might be at the bank, the supermarket, my local café…. But I'm confident that no matter when or where I do, I will look good.

But it takes money to look great, right? Absolutely not. There are lots of ways to dress up on a tight budget and I am about to share with you some of those secrets. Here are five frugal fashion tips for maximizing your style—and your REACH!—without maxing out your credit card.

1. **Be budget-friendly.** In my copy-making days at the mortgage company, I could not have expensive taste in clothing because I simply didn't have the money. Back then, all of my clothing came from large department stores. The good news is: You can absolutely put together attractive ensembles with a low investment if you are shopping in such stores because they most often follow the fashion industry's

lead. If Vogue says black is "in" this season, the clothing racks at Target and Walmart will carry black. The black pantsuit at Nordstrom is likely to be higher quality, but that doesn't matter when you're making impressions on people. The average person in your networking group or office will never know that your ensemble came from Target. Never. So don't pay extra for a tag that nobody's going to see or notice.

2. **Give your thrift shop a chance.** There was a woman I worked with for many years in the mortgage industry named Connie. She was an assistant to one of the other loan officers. She was tall, beautiful, and always wore amazing clothes—despite living on an assistant's salary. She had a revolving collection of designer suits that I always envied. One day, she let me in on her secret: thrift shops. She would drive out to the most affluent suburban communities and find their local consignment shops. There she had the opportunity to peruse the racks for her favorite designers. She amassed a closet full of top-notch designer suits and shoes for a fraction of their original cost. The result: Connie looked like she was stepping out of a fashion magazine each day she got to the office—and heads would always turn. If you are a brand snob or fixated on quality but can't afford high-end boutiques, thrift shops are the way to go. By the way, guys can find awesome thrift store finds too! In fact vintage is in and I have many fashion-forward male friends who love finding great vintage items at their local thrift stores.

3. **Be selective.** Most people have too many clothes. I am one of them. One reason is that I enjoy having a wide selection to choose from. But you don't need to wear a different outfit every single day for twelve months to create REACH!. If you have five sharp ensembles, you have the ability to

REACH!. That's one nice suit, or professional outfit per day for an entire workweek. REACH!ing through fashion is about creating a great first impression and about looking professional when it matters. Five suits is plenty for this purpose. If you are a woman, you will also need to add two black cocktail dresses for evening networking events and a couple of casual dress down outfits for weekend play and casual days. Men, you have it a bit easier; your casual collection just needs a couple nice Polo shirts or sweaters (depending on the season), plus two pairs of jeans with no holes or frayed bottoms.

4. **Accessorize.** The number one inexpensive way to add some spice to your wardrobe for very little money is accessories. Necklaces, bracelets, and earrings, oh my! For men, really fun cuff links can turn a plain old button-down shirt into a conversation starter. The best part about accessories is that it's really difficult to discern price. I have seen celebrities and power businesswomen alike spice up a cocktail dress with great costume jewelry that could easily cost $1,000 or $5. I always opt for lower-price accessories because I know that over time, I will grow bored of them and look for something new.

5. **Find your signature look.** I've always found it important to have a signature, go-to outfit when it comes to fashion, something you put on that always works and stands out from the rest. I grew up in the age of Laverne & Shirley and I loved that Laverne always wore her signature "L" on her chest. It's something we all came to look for (whether we realized it or not) to identify her. By creating a signature with your wardrobe, those around you will start to focus more on your signature, and less on whatever else you are wearing.

For example, when I attend networking events, I often have colleagues approach me and say, "Stacey, I saw you come in and I had to come see what shoes you picked tonight!" Suddenly my focus shifts from worrying about whether my slacks got wrinkled in the car or the button popped off my suit coat to showing off my shoes and creating more REACH! for myself. My fashion signature has always been wearing funky, distinct pairs of shoes. Back in high school, it was pink Chuck Taylors or patterned Doc Martins. Now my shoes mostly tend to be pumps. I have found that by wearing bright yellow patent-leather stilettos or deep purple velvet high-heeled penny loafers, I divert attention away from my outfit and down to my shoes. In instances where I prefer the attention to stay on my wardrobe, I select more toned down footwear like a pair of black leather shoes.

This principle applies to men as well. Donald Trump always wears a business suit. Rarely will you catch him wearing blue jeans—and never to work. His signature, however, is his *ties*. He is known for wearing ties with rich colors like cornflower blue, sunny yellow, and deep red. He is no stranger to playing with patterns as well. How can you make your run of the mill, boxy, blue pinstripe suit pop? Add a fun tie.

I have noticed in my twenty years in the business world that fashion is a universal language. It's something that we can all appreciate and duplicate to fit our own passions and lifestyles. Fashion is an instrument for recreating—and sometimes reinventing—who we are on the inside by piecing together physical representations of ourselves with clothing and accessories on the outside. Just like a smile can change your inner demeanor, so can a red bauble necklace that brings your plain black cocktail dress to life. Candy red stilettos and a black power suit make me feel confident that I can command a business lunch. A flowery sundress with flip-flops brings out the kid in me.

Fashion also gives us an outlet for transforming ourselves into millions of different characters throughout our lives. Like a chameleon changes colors, we can facilitate our ever-changing roles in life through fashion, from mom or dad, to salesperson, to business leader, to charity organizer, to fun-loving kid who loves the beach. We weave in and out of our roles and we experiment with new ones. Fashion accentuates the many faces of our individual lives. It's important that we choose clothes for all of these roles that make us feel confident so that we can be present in these moments and the best version of ourselves.

In 2013 my two closest girlfriends Christi, Ann Marie, and I decided to launch our own women's fashion business to capitalize on this idea that fashion is our opportunity to change our persona, often multiple times throughout a day. It is this idea that anyone can become the next Jackie O by throwing on a pink skirt suit and large oval-framed sunglasses. Our company, My Little Black Box (www.MyLittleBlackBox.com), is a subscription accessory service where women from around the world can sign up to receive new jewelry and other accessories every month. All pieces come in little black boxes. Here's the catch: Customers don't get to pick what they are getting. Rather than allow women to select pieces that reinforce their current identity, we encourage them to grow into the type of person that would wear, say, a crinkle scarf, a five-strand beaded bracelet, or trendy bauble earrings. We include a card inside each little black box that describes the type of woman that would wear its contents and we remind our customers that the woman we are talking about on the card lives in her, too. The goal is that adding this new accessory helps our customers add confidence as well.

Humans are so multi-dimensional, and fashion is a way to draw out the many sides that we all represent. When My Little Black Box launched, we weren't sure if women would understand what the point of our program was. Yet it took off so quickly that we could barely contain the initial flood of sign-ups we received. Apparently women totally appreciate what we are offering, a chance to discover new styles and the exciting new confidence that comes with them.

Now, if you are a guy reading this section, your first thought is probably, "This doesn't apply to me. Men don't have all these personas within us; that's a 'girl' thing!" But there's one really big accessory that men worldwide seem to have taken to that would suggest otherwise. It's not cufflinks or a really cool belt. No, the accessory that many men have fallen in love with to bring out their inner warrior is called a Harley Davidson.

According to the Harley Davidson website, the average owner of a Harley motorcycle between 2002 and 2006 was a 46-year-old man with an average income of $81,000. In fact 90 percent of Harley owners during this timeframe were male. Harley Davidson is a company that has mastered its marketing. It targets doctors, lawyers, accountants, and other professionals who have a little bit of renegade in them.

Furthermore, Harley does more than market a bike–it's selling you on a *lifestyle*. Its ads promise you more freedom, open roads, and adventure. Plus, there's the added bonus of camaraderie with like-minded adventure seekers through more than 1,400 HOGs (Harley

Owner Groups) worldwide. They're all listed on the Harley website along with upcoming conventions and rallies near you.

What's a Harley have to do with fashion? Everything.

By its definition, fashion is a popular trend, especially in styles of dress, ornament, or behavior. Guys own Harleys for the same reason girls like me wear stiletto shoes, fun accessories, and little black dresses: We are all equally seeking outward expressions of who we perceive ourselves to be at that moment in time.

Even if you can't get past the idea that a motorcycle is no different than a pair of fire engine red Jimmy Choo shoes, consider this: In 2012, Harley Davidson customers spent $4.9 billion. Most of that money paid for motorcycles, parts and bike accessories, and yes, fashion accessories. Harley raked in $299.4 million in general merchandise like shirts, jeans, jewelry, vests, and other goods emblazoned with its logo. At $4.9 billion, Harley generated more revenue than several top women's clothing giants saw in 2012 including Michael Kors ($2.1 billion) and The Jones Group, parent to brands like Jones New York, Nine West, and Easy Spirit ($972 million).

The Harley Davidson bike and merchandise represent the cool guy, the free bird, the renegade, whatever persona enables its owner to tap into a new level of confidence. And whether that confidence comes from a leather seat or leather pumps, it enables men and women around the world to create REACH! into networks of others like them and the right attitude to REACH! for their greatest dreams and ambitions in all areas of their life.

It seems as though more and more men are realizing what an important role fashion plays in their REACH!. My fiancée, Jay, owns a successful real estate firm and appreciation marketing business. In

2012, one of Jay's clients introduced him to a men's custom clothing company called J.Hilburn. He only agreed to go in and get measured for clothing because his client happened to be a salesperson there, and he felt he owed it to her to try out her product. Today, Jay is a J.Hilburn fanatic.

I know when Jay has an important meeting coming up because he's usually looking around his closet frantically for one of his J.Hilburn shirts. He says he loves the way the shirts fit him perfectly and how the fabric feels against his skin. He also says they help him stand out at networking events because their colors never seem to fade. Whether or not those things are true, all that matters is that Jay feels more confident when he's wearing a J.Hilburn shirt. Feeling good equates to confidence, which means a great attitude, and a passion to succeed, all of which give him the power to REACH!.

It's easier to REACH! when you feel good about yourself. It takes a healthy dose of self-esteem to achieve your wildest dreams in life. So if REACH!ing for a new pair of shoes, a great necklace, or even a motorcycle offers you the confidence you need to create REACH!, do it.

For me, fashion has created REACH! in one other important way: It has served as an icebreaker on several occasions, especially when it comes to—you guessed it—my shoes. For instance, I have found that when I wear a pair of crazy shoes to a networking function, nine times out of ten someone will come over to me and say, "I love those shoes!" This typically creates a dialogue about where I got the shoes, where the best shoe stores are, and exchanging stories about shoes. Before you know it I've established a genuine bond with someone I wanted to meet. I also find myself scanning the crowd for another cool pair of shoes because I know when I've found them, there's a woman standing in them who is totally speaking my language. I never miss the opportunity to go and introduce myself to her by saying, "Where did you get those shoes? I love them!"

Is there really such a thing as physical beauty? In my opinion, it doesn't exist. Beauty is too subjective for enough of us to agree on an ideal appearance. I don't concentrate on my own physical looks because I know I can't change them substantially—and thankfully I have no inclination to. I also don't want my daughter to grow up thinking that her physical looks matter. There is one thing that we can all control, however, and that is our fashion. We can utilize clothing, accessories, and even motorcycles to offer the world an artistic peek into who we perceive ourselves to be on the inside. Therefore, fashion can portray—and even enhance—inner REACH!. But what we possess on the inside will always create the greatest REACH! of all.

REACH! Challenge

1. List three ways you could start dressing for the job you want, rather than the job you have.

2. Try adding a new twist to your fashion: a suit, a tie, or accessories you wouldn't normally try. Try something new every day for a week and journal your results. Are others treating you differently? Do you feel different? What do you like about the change? Commit to putting a little sizzle in your fashion to help you REACH! your goals.

3. At the next networking event, look for an opportunity to incorporate fashion into your REACH!. Break the ice by offering a compliment on someone's tie or shoes, for instance.

Visit www.REACHTools.net for free
downloadable REACH! resources.

Chapter 11

Love

"Reach for the stars." – Christa McAuliffe

I was thirty-five years old when I found the man I wanted to spend the rest of my life with. If you are sitting back waiting for love to find you, you might be waiting a long time. And if you aren't willing to REACH!, there's a good chance you will never get what you want.

I grew up in a society where girls weren't supposed to ask guys out. It was the other way around. So I sat back and waited for dates. I almost didn't go to my own prom until my best friend's brother did me a favor and asked me to go with him. It had never occurred to me back then that I could actually REACH! and ask for what I wanted. Maybe if I had reached back then, life would be different today. The opposite of REACH! is to sit and wait for things you want. This is a poor strategy. It's a strategy that will land you with your best friend's brother doing you a favor by taking you to the prom. Today, I would never wait for the love of my life to come along and fall into my lap. I've had plenty of those guys. If they are flinging themselves at you, rest assured, there's a reason—and it's probably more for their benefit than yours.

There's a perfect mate out there for you. Only you can know what the perfect match for you would be. I created mine in my head and even wrote down his qualities on paper. By the time I met him in real life, I knew right away that I found him and I REACH!ed for him!

It takes guts to REACH! for the guy or gal you like. I know; I've done it myself and have been rejected more times than I can count. The only thing worse than rejection, however, is sitting back and waiting. With rejection, at least you are pursuing a relationship you are interested in. By sitting and waiting, you are more likely to settle for what you get. Why settle when all you need to do is REACH!?

Prior to meeting Jay, I dated on and off while busily pursuing other passions. Sometimes my personal relationships would last a while; others would last just a date or two. One relationship lasted for more than ten years until I finally decided that my happiness required me to REACH! to pull myself out of it.

When it comes to finding love and happiness there are five key strategies that have worked for me.

1. **REACH! beyond your comfort zone.**

If you are anything like me, you tend to stop reaching when relationships don't work. It's tiring to date person after person and never find the right match, so you constrict and conform. Instead of continuing to look for Miss or Mr. Right, you tend to settle for someone with whom you are not compatible. The result in these situations is that someone needs to change. You either conform the best you can or you try to change the other person. I've been in both types of situations.

In one instance I just kept trying to convince myself that I needed to work harder to be the person that my partner wanted me to be. Any friends of mine who were courageous enough to point out that I was changing for the worse became "Public Enemy No. 1" to my partner. He would discourage me from spending time with them, even insisting that I stop talking to some of them altogether. By the way, anyone who tries to prevent your positive REACH! by closing off your networks, especially with friends you have known for years, is probably not a good fit for you. It's been my experience that people who try to prohibit REACH! do so because they lack REACH! themselves. It's likely that your REACH! scares them because they don't want to lose the only one they have REACH! with—you! Also someone who lacks the capacity to REACH! for his or her own big, audacious goals in life is often the same type that is a naysayer when you REACH! for yours.

I have also been in a relationship where I tried to change the other person. I was in a long-term engagement throughout my twenties with a guy named Mark. He was a nice guy but not as driven by work as me. We had different goals from the beginning, and I tried to change his for many years before realizing that sometimes REACH! requires you to take an uncomfortable step out of a relationship that just is not meant to be.

The longer people convince themselves to stay in bad matches, the more comfortable and predictable their lives seem, whether it's good for them or not. REACH! beyond what's comfortable and pursue what you really want out of love. Don't give up after a failed relationship, or even a string of them. Look at the broken pieces of each failed partnership, figure out what you each could have done better, and what the warning signs were. That way, you will be able to judge people and your relationships better moving forward.

I met my fiancée Jay by stepping out of my comfort zone. I asked him out even though it was uncomfortable and unfamiliar—even though I knew in my heart he would say no. He said yes and the rest is history.

2. **Find a match who supports your REACH!.**

What matters most in any relationship is that both sides are clear about their goals; relationship goals, family goals, business goals, and life goals. Your goals don't have to be the same, nor do your ways of pursuing them. I've seen long-term relationships work out for the best when both people are total opposites of one another. But you and your partner need to buy into and support each other's goals. Otherwise, trouble is on the horizon.

The trouble with goals is that they change. I don't know about you, but my life and business goals have changed more times than I can count. That's why it's important to discuss goals with your partner or potential partner from day one. If you haven't had this type of conversation with your partner lately, today's the best day to do it. This exercise works best when done simultaneously with your partner so you can share ideas about how you will help one another REACH! for your dreams. Make sure to take this challenge quarterly to be better aware of when one or both of your dreams have altered.

REACH! is so much easier when you have a partner working with you to get there. I have been lucky to end up with a partner who promotes my REACH! most of the time. No matter what I am REACH!ing for next, he's beside me cheering me on. What does one do when they have a partner who doesn't support their REACH!? The first option (and best in my opinion) is to question why your partner is not supporting your REACH!. Does your partner feels threatened that you will leave him or her behind when you accomplish your goal? Is it because you didn't help your partner REACH! for something that was important to him or her? If your relationship is important to you, then you should try to get to the bottom of why there is no support for your REACH!. If you can get to the bottom of it, there's a good chance you will end up with a partner cheering you on as you go after your dream.

Every once in a while, I will go to REACH! for something in my life and Jay will say, "That's a bad idea." I always take a step back and reevaluate because sometimes he's totally right. The second option is to choose not to REACH! after all. Perhaps your partner is completely right, that REACH!ing is a bad idea, and after a thoughtful conversation you can see why. In such instances, it's ok to go with your gut. If it's telling you to hold back, then simply choose not to REACH! right now. Always err on the side of REACH!. Go for it, unless your gut is screaming for you to hold back.

The third option is to move forward without that person's support—and that's ok sometimes. You won't always have 100 percent support from every person in your life. If you want something bad enough, you should REACH! for it anyway.

Look around you. Everything you have in your life—your relationships, house, car, job, kids, you name it—is the result of your REACH!. There will always be people who have more than you, and the only difference between you and them is their REACH!. They were willing to REACH! for more than you and/or more often. REACH! is responsible for everything good you have in your life. Therefore, I hope you protect your REACH! as if it were a 5 carat diamond. Don't ever let someone else control your REACH!. And when someone tries to, be very leery. When you REACH! your way into a relationship that supports your REACH!, you will achieve your dreams faster and with less hassle than if you go it alone.

3. **Love is a process, not a destination.**

I'm in a great relationship with someone whom I consider to be my best friend. Are there days that he drives me crazy? Definitely. I'm sure I drive him equally crazy. Are there even days that I think I would be better off alone? Yes. Regardless, he is my happy ending. Life is not a movie. There's no such thing as: "Stacey meets Jay. Stacey asks Jay out. They fall in love and have a baby together. The end." It's not quite that easy. A relationship works when everyone realizes that a loving relationship is an ongoing process of give and take.

There are times in my life when I need to modify my REACH! so that I can better support Jay's. He has goals too, as does our three-year-old daughter for that matter. I can't expect Jay to be my cheerleader all the time, unless I'm willing to be his too. I can't look for him to support my lofty business goals if I don't support what he's working on in his career. The REACH! we each create in our own lives is a product of our primary relationships with those who support us. This means that our REACH! is not only a product of the effort we put into our own goals, but it is equally a product of the REACH! we put into the goals of others. What I am suggesting here is that to REACH! faster and further, you will need a support system of people who will help you. It starts at home: Your spouse, partner, children, and/or roommates will be integral in your REACH! equation. Without their support, it will simply take longer to get where you want to go. And if you expect support from your family, then you must support them in their REACH! too.

What should you do when a loved one is REACH!ing toward something you don't agree with? Explain your concerns, and then support them anyway. Your unconditional support not only demonstrates your commitment to their life dreams, but it also benefits your own REACH!. Remember the equation we talked about: Your own personal REACH! is a product of not just your effort but the effort that your support system puts in as well. You can't expect unconditional support if you aren't willing to give it.

4. "Know when to hold 'em, know when to fold 'em…"

Kenny Rogers' lyrics make for timeless advice when it comes to relationships. It's important to maintain relationships with people who positively benefit your REACH!, confidence, and quality of life—and end or redefine the ones with those who don't. When should you hold onto a relationship and when should you let one go? The answer is different for everyone. Only you know when you have given it your all and need to step away. Here are some questions to consider:

- Have you offered unconditional support for his/her REACH!?

- How might your relationship change if s/he accomplishes his/her goal?

- Has s/he unconditionally supported your REACH!?

- Were you clear about your goals?

- Was s/he clear about his/her goals?

- Did you talk to him/her about why s/he doesn't support your REACH!?

- Based on what you have invested in the relationship so far, would it be worth hiring a third-party counselor to discuss how you two can better support one another?

Consider writing out a pros-and-cons list for both staying in and getting out of your questionable relationships. As well, consider both the short-term and long-term repercussions of holding or folding. For example if you stay in a particular relationship, what do you think your life will look like in one year, five years, and ten years from now? And what will life look like in one, five, and ten years if you get out of it? Of course life offers many twists and turns, and there's no guarantee that your predictions will be 100 percent accurate. But when it comes to considering the benefits of your relationships, REACH!ing to the future for a best guess of what the repercussions will be is a good idea.

5. **It's never too late.**

It's never, never, *never* too late to build relationships. I have many friends who are quite content without a spouse or significant other in their lives—and that's great if it's what you want. But if you do seek companionship, don't stop REACH!ing for it. You are not too old, too tired, too busy, too whatever. If you focus on finding a great partner and you REACH! by trying new ways of finding love, the right partner will come along. As well, keep building your networks because the more you have, the better your chances of finding a great match will be.

Remember, I was thirty-five years old before I met Jay. I had tried online dating sites. I graciously accepted blind dates set up by friends. But it was my own network that eventually brought me a partner with whom I was totally compatible. I met Jay at a real estate conference where I was teaching. I was out creating greater REACH! for my business and I ended up finding someone whom I can now REACH! with for the rest of my life.

Aside from Jay, I've also found that having great friendships outside the home also helps enhance your ability to REACH!. For me, my girlfriends offer me respite from home life when I need it. We each share our REACH! struggles with one another and we do our best to offer sound advice or a shoulder to lean on when needed. My friends work hard to maintain balance in work and life and it helps to share our struggles with each other.

My good friend Christina runs several businesses with her partner Eric in Hawaii. There are major challenges whenever you mix business and the pleasure of living in a vacation destination, but they manage to keep their lives balanced and their focus where it needs to be (either business or rest) at any given time. Christina feels centered when she's at home with Eric, and so she's willing to REACH! when it comes to maintaining a balance in their work life too.

My friend and business partner Ann Marie and her husband Jeff work opposite schedules: He works all night and sleeps by day while Ann Marie works all day and sleeps by night. They never see each other enough, but they REACH! for the common good of their family and spend weekends together as much as possible.

My other friend and business partner Christi and her husband Ryan have three kids and they each balance a handful of jobs. Together they run a farm that sells Christmas trees in the winter and flowers in the spring. They are the local go-to spot for seasonal gifts for every major holiday throughout the year. In addition, Ryan runs a construction business and Christi has her own fashion line, Clutch!, writes for *The Huffington Post*, and co-owns www.mylittleblackbox.com with myself and Ann Marie. Christi and Ryan balance their hectic lives by sharing in the work at home. They share the burden of carpooling kids to daycare and to appointments, and both are willing to sacrifice in order to help the other achieve personal goals. They also commit to spending at least one date night out each month.

Love is a process, not a destination. It takes work to foster great relationships. My closest girlfriends and I have all learned that finding the perfect match at home enables us to live busy lives complete with kids, families, and multiple businesses with minimal stress, maximum productivity, and maximum joy.

REACH! Challenge

Who are the five people you are closest with? Over the next five days, contact each of the five and let them know that you are reading this book and that it caused you to think about them. Ask each one what big goals they are working on in their lives right now and what one thing you could do to support them in their REACH!. There are four keys to successfully completing this challenge:

1. Don't make this conversation about you. Your goal is to simply find out how you can help them.

2. Make sure your support for their REACH! goal is communicated. You want your people to know that they have a cheerleader rooting them on.

3. When they offer ideas on how you can help them achieve their REACH!, follow through and take action.

4. REACH! back regularly to follow up on their goals until they have achieved them.

Remember the REACH! equation: Every time you help others achieve their goals, you move closer to achieving your own.

Visit www.REACHTools.net for free downloadable REACH! resources.

Chapter 12

REACH![3]

"Asking is the beginning of receiving. Make sure you don't go to the ocean with a teaspoon. At least take a bucket so the kids won't laugh at you." – Jim Rohn

Asking results in REACH! cubed. Nothing will assist you in creating your dreams and accomplishing your goals faster than asking, especially when you get stuck. This requires asking for what you want, even when it's uncomfortable to do so. The bottom line is that you can sit back, take small strides, and wait for what you want, or you can go out and ask for it and get it now.

Here are three keys to creating REACH![3] by asking.

1. **Identify who or what stands between you and your dream.**

Really, there is only a "who" between you and your dream. In other words, there is definitely someone out there who can assist you in REACH!ing your goal. These people come in two main types: direct connectors who can directly assist you in the achievement of your goal; and indirect connectors who can connect you to—you guessed it—the direct connectors.

There is no "what" between you and your REACH!. You might feel like there is some inanimate, non-living thing that is stopping you from getting to where you see yourself or your business in the future (i.e., a lack of investment capital). But when you peel back the layers of that "what," you will find a "who" (i.e., someone who can supply or help you raise the capital you need).

Bob Mason has opened my eyes to the world of angel investing and venture capital partnerships. He is a mentor for TechStars, a company that helps startup businesses go from conception to launch, assisting with everything from venture capital fundraising to software development. TechStars is in the business of creating optimum REACH! for the businesses it mentors.

According to its website, TechStars is the number one startup accelerator in the world. Because of its reputation and REACH!, it receives thousands of applications each year, but only a handful are selected. You are more likely to get accepted into an Ivy League college than to have your startup accepted into TechStars' mentoring program. But if you get in, let's just say that your REACH! gets cubed—and then some. Mentees receive $18,000 in seed funding and an optional convertible debt note of $100,000. But after the program, they raise an average $1.6 million in outside venture capital.

I have always started my businesses small, adding one new operations employee, one new salesperson, or one new office at a time. This is fine for many entrepreneurs who are happy with limited growth. However, if you want to grow quickly, venture capital and angel funds may be the way to go.

I embarked on a journey to learn all I could about venture capital funding and angel investing because I came to the realization, after having built my real estate firm to 14 offices, that there had to be a way to grow this business, and future ones, faster. As I did, one concept in particular stuck out to me: Many entrepreneurs launch businesses using venture capital funds even if they don't need the money. But why would those with millions sitting in the bank use other people's money to launch a business if they had plenty to do it on their own? The answer is simple: It creates REACH![3]. It turns out that when you give others a stake in your business, you create partners who are now equally committed to making sure your business succeeds. After all, they now want to make sure they get a return on their investment in it.

Perhaps it's not money that you lack, but rather confidence to go after your dream. Confidence also seems like a "what" barrier that actually has a "who" solution: There are people in the business of building confidence. You just have to REACH! out to them—or an indirect connector who knows them. They are coaches, consultants, and even therapists who make their living by helping others build the confidence they need to achieve REACH!. Invest your time and money in someone who is willing to help you map out a plan for achieving your goals and who can help you overcome fear and adversity along the way. If getting coached is not for you, consider finding an accountability partner, someone who can help you outline your own goals and milestones and hold you accountable for REACH!ing them.

Rest assured, there is never just a "what," an inanimate object standing between you and your REACH!. There is always someone who can guide you to your destination. Your mission, should you choose to accept it, is to find those people and ask them for the assistance you need to REACH!.

2. **Figure out why you haven't asked yet.**

Right this very moment, you are making a decision about your

REACH!. You are either deciding to take the long road or the short one. If you are sitting on the long road, the only thing preventing you from getting on the short one is your ability to ask. People who achieve all of their dreams spend the better part of each day asking. In sales, we call it prospecting. If you spend two or three hours a day prospecting for business, you are on the short road to accomplishing your dream. The more times you ask for what you want each day, the faster you will REACH! your destination.

Here are some quick tips to help you become a more effective asker:

a) *Get replies now, not later.* In sales and entrepreneurship, there are a few ways to ask for what you want. One way is the belly-to-belly approach where you physically get in front of the person you need help from and ask for what you want. This is the most effective way to REACH! because you get an answer right now. Of course it is also the most intimidating because you risk getting rejected right now, too. But believe it or not, you will have a higher success rate when dealing directly with someone in person (or on the phone, if absolutely necessary). That's because as hard as it is for you to take rejection, it's even harder for someone else to dish it out. You don't like rejecting people when they ask for something, right? Isn't it easier to help them with what they need than to flat-out reject them? Of course it is. Just the same, the people you ask in person will be more inclined to help you. And what if someone turns you down? Hard as it may be to take that rejection, it's important to get that answer right away so you can move on to your next prospective connector. If you give someone the opportunity to delay rejecting you, you could lose a lot of time that should have been spent finding the right help.

If you already spend your days asking but you are not getting anywhere, than I am willing to bet that you are trying to create REACH! with a "reply later" ask, marketing your business, idea, or goal through mailings, social media, and other indirect marketing campaigns. Small business owners spend thousands of dollars prospecting through these channels so they won't have to hear the word "no"; people can just choose to ignore your mailing or tweet—and 99.99 percent of them will. While mailings, social media, and other outreach activities can help you cultivate relationships and maintain credibility, they're most often not the best avenues for an ask. If you are seriously driven to achieve a long-term goal, make a personal connection, or land a sale, you need to spend a majority of your time belly to belly with people who can reply now.

b) *It's not about you.* There are two ways to ask for what you want: You can make the ask about you, or you can make it about the other person. Whenever possible, make it about the other person. Here are some examples:

ABOUT YOU: "I was wondering if you might need a refill on my product."

ABOUT THEM: "I wanted to reach out and share a special we are offering with you."

ABOUT YOU: "I'm looking for referrals."

ABOUT THEM: "I wanted to reach out to see if you have any friends who might need help pricing a home right now."

ABOUT YOU: "I saw you are in need of new employees, and that's the business I am in."

ABOUT THEM: "I saw your article about your workforce expansion and wanted to extend some help since I am in the talent recruiting business."

Try to lace your asks with "you" and "your" rather than "me" and "my." And always emphasize how you can help them, not how they can help you.

Sometimes, it's just not possible to make an ask about them. In such instances, still make the ask, but explain why you are asking them specifically, rather than just anyone, and express your appreciation for their assistance. This gratitude will help warm them up to you and your request.

c) *Go for "No."* Andrea Waltz and Richard Fenton wrote a simple yet remarkable book entitled *Go for No!* about how your ability to achieve any goal is directly proportionate to the number of nos you are willing to take. You don't like rejection? Get over it. The only possible way to achieve anything in life is to walk through the valley of No. You might not hear a "no" while you're down there, but chances are you will. The most successful people aren't the ones who manage to avoid "no"; they're the ones who welcome them and trudge through them until they hear the "yes" they're REACH!ing for. The best way to develop the thick skin needed in this valley is to hear "no" more often. So challenge yourself to reach a certain number of nos every single day. Before you know it, you will be hearing more yeses and be well on your way to REACH!ing your dreams.

3. **Realize what will happen if you don't ask.**

Asking can be scary. The risk of rejection is scary, and rejection itself can deflate your much-needed confidence if you're not properly trained to accept it and move on. But if you don't ask, will you be stuck where you are right now next week, next month, next year? If so, how much more could that stagnation cost you? The answer is lots of your time, the chance to obtain all you desire, and the experience of dealing with rejection and moving past it.

Sure, there's an off chance that someone will come along and lend a hand without you asking, but what are the chances of that? And why should anyone help you if you are not willing to help yourself? If you are so indifferent about your dream that you don't have the guts to ask for what you want, I know that I wouldn't want to go out on a limb to help you. Why would I? Why should anyone else?

If that sounds a bit harsh, it should. I hope it comes across as unforgiving, because life is unforgiving to those who lack REACH! and the ability to ask for help. I further hope that these tips spur you to ask more. Looking back on all the REACH! I've achieved so far, the ability to ask for what I want has been the bedrock of my success. Each business I have built started with a simple plan, documenting a start point, an end point, and a list of asks I need to make along the way.

I started my real estate firm in 2001 with eleven agents. Ten years later, it grew to three hundred agents—in one of history's bleakest real estate markets. How did I achieve that? I made it a habit to pick up the phone and ask great agents to join my firm. If I didn't ask, why would they join? Maybe a few would have found their way here on their own. But for the most part, most people are not going to consider jumping to my company—or any for that matter—without an invitation. The most important part of my business plan is *ask*.

In fact, asking is so vitally important to my business that it's the first thing I do when I get to the office each day. I make my asks early in the morning to get them out of the way. Why? Because asking is hard work! Even for experienced askers, making a strong ask takes planning, consideration of what the other person wants or needs, and the energy to actually have the conversation and make a compelling case. If I don't do it first thing each day, I might not get it done. I ask early and often. I never get insulted by a no. And I never consider "no" to be someone's final answer.

Another person who has mastered asking is my friend and business partner Ann Marie who started working part time as a real estate agent in 2002 while still working in the corporate tech industry. She sold twenty-five houses that year. On top of countless private showings, she conducted an open house every Sunday and attended networking events after her day job, always making sure to ask each person if they or anyone they knew was in need of real estate expertise. In her first year, Ann Marie REACH!ed out whenever she could to get her feet wet in the industry. As a result, she quickly became a top agent in her area over the next eight years, selling upwards of one hundred fifty houses per year—all while managing a team of agents.

In 2010, Ann Marie was pregnant with her second child and desired for a more stable environment for her family both financially and on a daily scheduling basis. Her husband took a promotion that involved him working second shift, leaving their home early in the evening for work only to return early in the morning. They decided together that Ann Marie would go back to the corporate environment for the first time in more than six years. She was slightly nervous that she wouldn't be offered a job due to both her long absence from the corporate world *and* her being eight months pregnant. But bravely she started tapping into her network, making calls, asking for the jobs she wanted, and asking her personal connections to make introductions to people at the companies she was interested in working. Then, off she went on several interviews that lasted up to four hours—and her REACH! paid off! She didn't just receive one job offer, she received three and ultimately accepted a sales and marketing position working with c-level executives… the day before she went into labor.

Studies on rejection suggest that it takes an average of four nos in order to get one yes. In other words, to get a sale, you will have to contact the average potential client five times to get the answer you are looking for. And yet, according to Marketing Wizdom, 92 percent of salespeople give up before that fifth ask:

- 44% of salespeople give up after one "no"

- 22% give up after two

- 14% give up after three

- 12% give up after four

This means that only 8 percent of salespeople are still in the game by that critical fifth ask, where roughly half all of yeses wait for the taking. Are you in that 8 percent? You should be.

And four nos is just the average. Some of the Realtors who have joined my firm said no more than *twenty* times before signing on. I never badgered; I always followed up respectfully. But I always followed up. When it comes to building your own ask strategy, I encourage you to consider the same approach.

Oftentimes in sales, people reject your pitch simply because they're not ready to buy right now. Therefore, make sure to space out your asks over time so as not to badger, annoy, and eventually alienate your connectors. In my business, every three months works well. Find what length of time works best to help keep you in your connectors' consciousness. That way, you are next in mind when they are ready to help you or buy what you're selling.

Here is an example of how I employed the asking strategies we've just reviewed.

I enjoy blogging about how to build successful businesses and have built a great following around my three business blogs: www.StaceyAlcorn.com, www.MyLittleBlackBox.com, and www.P3Coaching.com. But in 2012, I resolved to REACH! for a more global audience and become a blog writer for *The Huffington Post*. I started researching how I would go about being considered and was surprised to find very little guidance online. I did come up with an email address at *Huffington* for submitting blog content, so I started writing posts and submitting them. No response. I kept submitting. No response. (Getting no answer is worse than rejection, in my opinion. At least with rejection you know where you stand.)

What was standing between me and my goal? As I covered at the beginning of this chapter, it's always a "who," not a "what," that's preventing you from accomplishing your dream. So to become a *Huffington Post* contributor, I knew I was going to have to start asking for help. The logical start was to find people already doing what I wanted to do. I needed to reach out to other blog writers who were already published on *Huffington.* I did not personally know anyone who was writing for them, so I started REACH!ing out to strangers. No response. Determined to accomplish my goal by the end of 2012, I even continued submitting content to the *Huffington* email I'd found in hopes for a breakthrough, but to no avail. As the leaves started falling from the trees in late fall, nobody seemed to want to help and I was getting anxious.

In late November, one of my real estate agents sent me a link to attend the seventh annual Massachusetts Conference for Women. The keynote speaker? Arianna Huffington. Now if there was one "who" who could help me blog for *The Huffington Post*, it was Arianna Huffington. I needed to speak to her directly.

I attended the one-day conference in early December with every intention of speaking with Arianna. I knew this would be a challenge since this conference attracted 10,000 women from across the state. But I knew this was my one shot, my one opportunity to REACH!. Arianna gave her keynote address during lunch. After that, she would be in the main hall signing books. While 10,000 women were working on their salads and socializing, I went and asked conference personnel where Arianna would be doing the book signing. I purchased a handful of her books and went to wait at the signing table before she arrived. I was the fifth person in line. After the luncheon, Arianna made her way to the book-signing table. My heart was racing. This was so much more than a book signing for me. I was about to REACH!.

Knowing the importance of making an ask about the other person, I thought hard about how I could frame my ask with Arianna. How could I make this about her? Surely, Arianna Huffington needs nothing from me. But right as my turn came, I figured out a way:

ARIANNA: "Hi Darling, what's your name?"

ME: "Stacey Alcorn."

ARIANNA: "How do you want me to sign your books?"

ME: "Just your name. I will give them out to clients and friends. Arianna, as a business owner, I would want to know if some of my systems weren't working. Do you feel the same?"

ARIANNA: "Of course."

ME: "I wanted to let you know that I have submitted blog content on your site for the past year and I have never once received a reply. I don't mind if I get rejected, but I don't even know if anyone is receiving my posts."

ARIANNA: "What do you do for work, Darling?"

ME: "I own several businesses including real estate offices, a law firm, and a consulting company."

ARIANNA: "Of course you should be writing for me. Take my card and contact me tomorrow."

With that Arianna handed me her business card. Within twenty-four hours I was a contributing blogger for *The Huffington Post*. I dreamed, stretched for, and achieved my goal. I now write monthly for *The Huffington Post* at www.HuffingtonPost.com/Stacey-Alcorn.

What is important to understand here is the process. First, I realized there was a "who" standing between me and my goal. At first I thought that the "who" was another *Huffington Post* blogger who could assist me in achieving my REACH! but I ultimately realized that the real "who" who could make my dream a reality was Arianna Huffington herself. Second, I didn't approach Arianna with an ask that was about me. I made it about her. I offered her feedback to help her create better systems for placing content on her site. Third, I didn't give up. After reaching out to many *Huffington Post* bloggers, none of whom were willing to REACH! back to me, I could have easily given up and chalked up the loss. Instead, I persevered. I simply kept REACH!ing until I got what I wanted.

I asked you earlier to consider the consequences of not asking. For me the consequence would have been never having the opportunity to expand my REACH! by millions through *The Huffington Post*. When I considered my REACH! from that perspective, I was willing to risk the pain of rejection from Arianna Huffington to go after what I really wanted. Remember, a little bit of rejection is good for the soul—as is getting what you really want out of life.

REACH! Challenge

1. Pull out your REACH! goals that you formulated at the beginning of our journey together.

2. Underneath each goal, write a list of the "who"s standing between you and your goal.

3. Underneath each "who," write an ask that is framed in such a way that you make the request about them, not you.

4. Write out a minimum of five dates during which you will ask for what you want.

5. Write out what will happen if your ask is successful.

6. Write out what will happen if you don't ask.

7. REACH!!

Visit www.REACHTools.net for free downloadable REACH! resources.

Chapter 13

Appreciate

*"Develop an attitude of gratitude, and give thanks for
everything that happens to you, knowing that every step
forward is a step toward achieving something bigger and
better than your current situation." – Brian Tracy*

Appreciation is the recognition of the quality, value, significance, or magnitude of people or things. Strong networks cannot be built without appreciation. It is the glue that will hold your network together tightly, creating stronger advocates for one another. Show your appreciation for these people and they will support you no matter what.

As I covered in Chapter 12, you can magnify your power of REACH! by asking for what you want, achieving REACH![3.] Well most of the time, your asks will involve REACH!ing out to people within your network. You are far more likely to get the assistance you seek when you truly appreciate the people around you—and genuinely express that appreciation. The two go hand in hand. It is useless to express appreciation when you don't feel it on the inside because such an expression will come off as canned and insincere. As well, appreciating people without expressing it to them is often no better than not appreciating them at all. Creating a strong REACH! dictates that appreciation be a two-step process. Appreciate others from your core and then express it to the person you appreciate.

Have you ever felt unappreciated by someone? Most of us have at some point. How do you feel about the person who doesn't appreciate you? You probably aren't going out of your way to advocate for that person. Now how would you feel if that person asked you for a favor, or to REACH! on his or her behalf? You might feel downright used, right? Perhaps you will begrudgingly try to help that person, but you are not going to put in any extra effort.

This is why appreciation is so vital to creating REACH!. Without it your network is malleable, but when you open yourself up to appreciating others, you create an air-tight network of promoters, backers, and supporters who are vested in helping you achieve your REACH!.

Here are three keys to appreciating your people:

1. **Listen.**

We live in a busy world compared to the one our ancestors grew up in. One hundred years ago, people were limited in their ability to communicate with others by their geography. On a daily basis, most of them just talked to the people they ran into in their neighborhoods. It was easy to feel and show appreciation for others because networks were small and there was plenty of time to stop and really pay attention to people. This is not so easy in today's fragmented society. Sure, it's great that we can communicate with thousands, even millions of people each day through email and social networks. But we are listening to so many conversations simultaneously that it may feel virtually impossible to pay sincere attention to what any *one* person is saying.

Most people long to be heard. They want someone to really listen to them. If you can perfect your listening skills, you will never have trouble building a solid network. Listening does not even necessarily mean that you must offer an answer or advice. It only means truly understanding what the person is saying.

Dale Carnegie writes a great lesson on listening in one of my favorite all-time books, which I've already brought up in Chapter 3, *How to Win Friends & Influence People*. The book begins with the premise that if you can become a really good listener, you will become a people magnet:

"You can make more friends in two months by becoming interested in other people than you can in two years by trying to get other people interested in you."

> I believe we all need to heed this message. Today we have a tendency to talk a lot about ourselves because we want recognition and validation for what we think and do. As a result, we become less adept at listening to others. Of course, the best way to appreciate others is to listen to them. When attending networking functions, be the person who works the floor, listening to people. Introduce yourself to others and then start listening. Get intensely interested in each person who speaks with you. Ask questions. Avoid focusing the discussion on you. Before long, your network will begin to grow and strengthen.

I worked in the mortgage industry for more than ten years. Within two years of becoming a mortgage originator, I became a top producing salesperson in my industry, at one point closing more than 400 mortgage applications a year. Looking back on it today, I attribute my success to my listening skills. My appointments would often last two hours, not because we were talking mortgages, but because I loved really finding out who my clients were as people. I wanted to know where they grew up, how they chose the industries they were in, and what they did in their free time. I was fascinated with each person. As a result, my clients knew I cared for them as people, not as paychecks. They sensed that I genuinely appreciated them and their business—and my business thrived.

Listening to people can become a struggle in business, especially as your business grows. I can't listen to my firm's three hundred real estate agents the same way that I used to listen when it was just ten. Now listening takes on different forms, like surveys about where my employees want to have their Family Appreciation Day or what new tools my salespeople would like access to. Surveys are impersonal and never as effective as a conversation, but they still play an important role. When you survey someone, it communicates to that person that his or her opinion matters. In my business there are many ways we survey people, including services like www.SurveyMonkey.com, or by polling them through our company's private Facebook group. My partner and I still listen the old-fashioned way by visiting offices and talking to our people as much as possible. But it's important that we adapt to the size of our company and use other tools as well. No matter how big your business gets the most important advice I can offer is: Never stop listening.

2. **Take the time.**

The one thing that is always in limited supply is time. Spending yours with someone you care about is the highest form of appreciation there is. I will even go one step further and say that "technology disconnected" time is even better. That means no computer, phone, or iPad. Spend time *in person* with your spouse, kids, parents, friends, and coworkers as often as possible. And the best way to amplify your time with these important people is by not just talking to them, but by really listening to them.

Recently I was at a coffee shop enjoying a conversation with one of the real estate agents at my firm, Mealea. Prior to this conversation, all I really knew about her was from what I observed. I knew she was a dedicated mom, an avid reader, and a hard worker, balancing multiple jobs and volunteer positions. It wasn't until I took the time to talk with her in person that I learned about the drive behind her work ethic. I learned that Mealea had spent part of her childhood in a concentration camp, working as a child laborer. Her family risked life and limb to escape to a refugee camp, losing her father in the process. Against all odds, her mother, siblings, and two cousins made it to the refugee camp. They lived there for years before a refugee outreach organization selected them to come to Boston and start a new life. Mealea would later graduate from Wellesley College, a highly esteemed institution with graduates such as Nora Ephron, Madeleine Albright, and Hillary Clinton, and the last place a young girl growing up in a concentration camp would probably ever expect to attend.

By spending one-on-one time listening to Mealea, I realized she was more than just a motivated, determined young women; she's a woman with REACH! so incredible that there is nothing she can't accomplish. When you spend time with people, your relationship with and understanding of them becomes three-dimensional as you no longer speculate about who they are, but truly understand what they are made of.

When coaching sales professionals and business executives, I make sure they block time in their schedules to build and sustain their most important relationships. Much the same, time with your loved ones should be scheduled into your calendar with a pen. When a client seeks to take that appointment, you simply explain that you already have given that time to another client.

Spending time with those who are not close to lots of people is important, too. Volunteer at your local elderly housing. REACH! out to your local Big Brothers Big Sisters organization or others like it to spend time with kids. Speak to a local high school or university, or mentor a student in your trade or business. The more time you spend with someone, the greater your REACH! with that person becomes. You will have established a bond from understanding that person at a deeper level, thus deepening your relationship, and you will be armed with the knowledge to help that person achieve his or her greatest REACH! potential.

3. **Give a thoughtful card, note, or gift.**

While spending time with and listening to people is a perfect way to demonstrate your appreciation for them, you can't spend exorbitant amounts of time with every person. (This becomes truer the more your business, family, and/or other networks grow.) Therefore, it becomes incumbent to find other ways to express genuine appreciation. The simplest way is to send a note with your expression of gratitude. Think of the last time you received a note or card in the mail. Did you pull it out of the stack of bills and solicitations and open it right away? I bet you did! There's also a really good chance that you still have that card sitting on a shelf somewhere. Why? Because you love the gesture, that small act of appreciation that made your day.

I have always harbored an aversion to throwing away cards. During the holidays I plaster one wall in my kitchen with Christmas cards. When the holiday is over, I save them. It's really difficult to throw away a card that someone selected just for you, or a card with someone's family photo on it. Cards are such a simple form of appreciation, yet so few of us use them.

I send thousands of cards each year. Most of them are sent through a system called SendOutCards, www.MyRandomActsofCardness. com. I love this system because it allows me to personalize my cards with photos and personal notes from me. I can add gifts—my favorite is gourmet brownies—and the system keeps track of the thousands of people I've REACH!ed out to and when. It enables me to recognize birthdays and other life milestones of the salespeople, staff members, and other important people in my network.

In addition to SendOutCards, I also keep a box of actual notecards and a case of my favorite books by my office desk so that I can quickly send handwritten notes to people I've met or spoken to throughout the day. I do my best to send these notes out as soon as possible; all too often, life gets in the way and delayed acts of appreciation get pushed onto the back burner and forgotten.

Keep in mind that not all expressions of gratitude are created equal. For instance, how effective is your "Happy Birthday" message on someone's Facebook Wall? You are expressing your appreciation for them, yes, but is it being seen and remembered by that person above the hundred other messages that person is receiving? Instead of doing what everyone else is doing, try something different: Record a video and post that on your friend's Facebook Wall, send a handwritten card, or better yet send a personalized gift.

I always like to share the story of the copy machine representative, Jeff, who went above and beyond to capture my attention. Since I own many businesses, I get contacted every month by copy machine salespeople trying to sell me their services. I rarely return the calls.

But in 2012, Jeff managed to REACH! out and open up a dialogue between the two of us. He first sent me a FedEx package. It contained a notecard that explained he had recently read my book on time management. He had photocopied some time management articles that he hoped would spark my interest. He didn't ask for business in his note, but he included his business card so I knew he was in the copy machine sales business. In other words, he wanted to ask for my business but made sure to focus his ask on me, not him.

I was blown away. He was the only copy machine salesman who offered me something of value before asking for my business. And in addition, he demonstrated his appreciation for who I was by tailoring his gift specifically to my interests. This wasn't the only package I received from Jeff. Over the next year and a half, I received other packages from Jeff that each included a book or article, and I'm always excited to open them. While other copy machine sales representatives never even get a call back, Jeff has engaged me in dialogue, simply by demonstrating appreciation.

I have not yet had the opportunity to do business with Jeff. However, he is a top candidate when I do need a copy machine. The point here is that if you are in a sales business, you can position yourself as a top candidate for business by focusing on appreciating your potential client long before they need you. Develop the relationship first to put yourself in a position to reap the rewards of that relationship later.

In Chapter 7, I talked a lot about the power of social networking and how entrepreneurs like Gary Vaynerchuk have multiplied the power of their networks by using them to listen to their customers rather than just talk to them. As you think of ways to REACH! back to your friends, employees, and customers, consider reading the conversations they're having with others on their social networks and then using that information to send them a card or gift. There's a client who reports that she's been sick on her Facebook Timeline? Rather than wish her well on her public Wall, send a note. Your employee's son was voted class president? Send some flowers to the house. Stop talking so much on your social networks and start *listening*. Listen, and then REACH! back in a meaningful and genuine way.

There is a price to pay for not expressing your appreciation to others. If you don't outwardly appreciate your spouse, you may find yourself in divorce court. If you don't appreciate your kids, you may find yourself estranged. If you don't appreciate your employees, you will find it difficult to retain talent, which may result in a business that struggles to grow. If you don't appreciate your customers, they will leave to find a business that does. Even worse, they might broadcast their grievances to the world, encouraging others to leave you as well.

In 2008, Sons of Maxwell musician Dave Carroll said his $3,500 guitar was broken while in United Airlines' custody. He alleged that he heard a fellow passenger say that baggage handlers on the tarmac at Chicago's O'Hare International Airport were throwing guitars during his flight's layover on route to Omaha. After arriving in Omaha, Carroll discovered that the guitar was wrecked.

When Carroll reported the problem to United employees, he says they were indifferent. United later told him that the damages would not be covered since he didn't file a written report within twenty-four hours of the incident. Carroll felt that nobody at the airline appreciated his guitar, his feelings, or his complaint. So what did he do? Dave and his band wrote a song entitled "United Breaks Guitars"; it became an instant YouTube and iTunes sensation upon its release in July 2009. As of 2013, it has been viewed more than 13 million times on YouTube and has been turned into a book about how social media has changed the face of customer complaints forever.

Long story short: It pays to appreciate people, and it can cost you enormously if you don't.

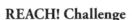

REACH! Challenge

1. Attend a networking event where you spend the entire time getting to know people. Refrain from discussing your own life or business and just get to know other people. Journal your results. Did you create greater REACH! by focusing on others or by sharing your own successes?

2. Operation Offline! Spend one hour per day with your family during which there are no "technoruptions." All mobile devices, computers, and tablets are to remain off. Make dinner together. Watch a movie. Play a board game. Talk. Spend time really listening to the people you love the most.

3. Next Monday, send a note expressing your appreciation to someone. On Tuesday send two notes. Wednesday, three notes. Thursday, four notes. Friday, five notes. In one workweek you will have sent a total of fifteen unanticipated cards of gratitude to people you appreciate. The following week, repeat with one note on Monday and so on. Do this for an entire month for a total of sixty expressions of gratitude. If you can do it for one whole year, that's 720 random acts of "cardness"! Your REACH! network will grow and strengthen which each card of appreciation you send.

Visit www.REACHTools.net for free
downloadable REACH! resources.

Chapter 14
Literary REACH!

"Reading is a discount ticket to everywhere." – Mary Schmich

If there's one thing that has influenced my life and my business more than anything over the past twenty years, it is this simple, fundamental activity: reading. I read books every single day, no matter what. I have a library full of books that I have consumed and an even larger collection waiting to be read. As author Brian Tracy once observed, "Did you ever notice that all the biggest, most beautiful homes have libraries?" The implication is that one key to financial success is reading. Don't just take my word for it; take Dana Gioia's. As the former chairman of the National Endowment for the Arts wrote in the NEA's 2007 report *To Read or Not to Read*:

"The shameful fact that nearly one-third of American teenagers drop out of school is deeply connected to declining literacy and reading comprehension. With lower levels of reading and writing ability, people do less well in the job market. Poor reading skills correlate heavily

with lack of employment, lower wages, and fewer opportunities for advancement. Significantly worse reading skills are found among prisoners than in the general adult population. And deficient readers are less likely to become active in civic and cultural life, most notably in volunteerism and voting…. The habit of daily reading… overwhelmingly correlates with better reading skills and higher academic achievement. On the other hand, poor reading skills correlate with lower levels of financial and job success."

Reading also does wonders for your REACH!. According to www.raisingbookworms.com, the website for Emma Walton Hamilton's book by the same name, literary readers are:

- Four times as likely to visit an art museum;

- Three times as likely to attend a performing arts event;

- Two-and-a-half times as likely to do volunteer or charity work;

- One-and-a-half times as likely to attend sporting events; and

- One-and-a-half times as likely to participate in sports activities.

In other words, reading heightens your desire to participate in the very social gatherings and networks that will increase your REACH!. In addition, everything you need to know how to REACH! for in life has already been written about. If you are looking for any answer, I guarantee it's in a book somewhere. REACH! is simply easier when you seek out clues along the way, and books are great places to find those clues. Unfortunately, most people just don't look for them there.

My own experience corroborates this. I owe much of my REACH! to books. They have given me comfort and guidance while getting over difficult losses in my life. They have helped me develop ideas and ambition when I have felt stuck. They have offered me hope and encouragement along my many journeys. They have even been some of my best advisors as I have grown multiple businesses. If you asked me whether books or my college education have had a greater impact on my successes, I would choose books without hesitation.

I often refer to my favorite authors as my own personal "board of directors" and give them credit for most of my business successes, including Napoleon Hill, Dale Carnegie, Steve Jobs, Warren Buffet, Daniel Pink, Sheryl Sandberg, Seth Godin, Ken Blanchard, Michael Gerber, and Tony Hsieh. Of course, I have not met nor spoken to most of these thought leaders, which is precisely the reason I share my story. Books and other media enable people to REACH! out and obtain advice, instruction, ideas, and even confidence from millions of people no matter what place—or time—they live in. All you have to do is decide what you want out of life and find books about it written by authors who have come before you.

I have never read a book I didn't enjoy and I believe that there is no such thing as a bad book.

I read all types of books, both fiction and non-fiction. It's important to read for pleasure now and again (my personal favorites are James Patterson and Janet Evanovich novels). But my favorite books cover inspiration, technology, and business. I also often read about topics that are totally outside the realm of my interests to see if they offer any unique insights to the businesses or other projects I am developing. For instance, I was never a big fan of history books, but I've picked up some very interesting pointers on business and leadership from biographies of great world leaders.

Ok, now you're convinced to start reading more. Great! But how do you decide *what* to start reading? I have created my own simple system for finding great books:

1. **Ask for recommendations from those you trust.** When I meet other business people, sales professionals, or authors, I always ask them what books they recommend. Most of the books I read were recommended by others. When someone offers me the name of a good book, I quickly make a note of it and order it within hours so that it's waiting on my bookshelf when I'm ready to read it.

2. **Order online.** I order most of my books from Amazon, which does a remarkable job of recommending books related to the ones I'm ordering. It's a great way to learn who else is writing about your topic of interest and quickly purchase their work as well. Plus, ordering online is faster and doesn't involve adding "drive to the store" to your already packed to-do list. The easier you make finding books for yourself, the more likely you will buy and read them.

3. **Visit library used book sales.** I make it a point to do this often. The one downside to Amazon is that it often forgets about great books that were published ten or twenty years ago and still offer timeless advice and ideas. Plus, you'll find many of these books at bargain prices. A few of my favorite books were bought on a dime—literally—at a used book sale, books like *The Richest Man in Babylon* by George S. Clason, *Profiles in Courage* by John F. Kennedy, and *Strength to Love* by Martin Luther King Jr. All three of these men have offered me golden nuggets of advice on managing multiple businesses, staying strong, and loving.

In my speeches, I like to remind attendees that I am not a doctor, but I do have the ability to heal most ailments in business and life. I heal by prescribing books. Give me your ailment and I will prescribe you a book that will offer you advice on how to correct your problem. I have prescribed thousands of books, often without being asked. I keep cases of books by my desk and send them out to people who need them. Not every book is read, I'm sure. But the ones that are—those are the ones that matter. When I prescribe a book and that book is read, I know that I have REACH!ed out into the world, into the life of someone else, and I have helped positively change the trajectory of that person's life forever.

One of my favorite books to prescribe is *The Compound Effect* by Darren Hardy. The reason it is one of my favorites is that it teaches you how to apply self-help principles in general, no matter what kind of help you need. For example, perhaps you have purchased a book on how to diet properly so you can lose weight, but you have yet to see results from that book. *The Compound Effect* helps you develop and implement a strategy for successfully using that other book's techniques and finally lose weight.

Each year, my office gets together and purchases one hundred Thanksgiving dinner baskets for local families in need. All of our team members pitch in money and the local supermarket helps us box up a complete turkey dinner for each family. In 2011, I included a copy of *The Compound Effect* in each basket. A turkey dinner will feed a family for one evening, but that book has the power to feed that family forever. I knew that not everyone would read the book, but what if just one person did? What would happen if a teenager in one of those families picks up the book and consumes it? What if I could change the trajectory of one person, one complete stranger, by arming him or her with a tome on how to achieve anything? Prescribing books—passing on other's wisdom—is a powerful and effective way to REACH!, so powerful in fact that I look for at least one opportunity per year to send books off into the world, into hands of complete strangers, in the sincere hope that someday someone will use their wisdom for good.

Here's a list of other books that will help you expand your REACH!. May you find their lessons useful and be inspired to pass them on to others as I have:

- *Predictably Irrational* by Dan Ariely

- *Focus* by Leo Babauta

- *Promptings* by Kody Bateman

- *The Power of Who* by Bob Beaudine

- *The One Minute Manager Meets the Monkey* by Kenneth Blanchard

- *Screw Business as Usual* by Richard Branson

- *Virus of the Mind* by Richard Brodie

- *Instant Rapport* by Michael Brooks

- *The Millionaire Messenger* by Brendon Burchard

- *Endless Referrals* by Bob Burg

- *The Go-Giver* by Bob Burg and John David Mann

- *The Secret* by Rhonda Byrne

- *The Success Principles* by Jack Canfield

- *How to Win Friends & Influence People* by Dale Carnegie

- *Don't Keep Me a Secret!* by Bill Cates

- *The Invisible Gorilla* by Christopher Chabris and Daniel Simons

- *Sales Encyclopedia* by John Chapin

- *The Richest Man in Babylon* by George S. Clason

- *Do More Faster* by David Cohen and Brad Feld

- *The 1% Solution for Work and Life* by Tom Connellan

- *How to Deliver a TED Talk* by Jeremy Donovan

- *The Power of Habit* by Charles Duhigg

- *Time Traps* by Todd Duncan

- *Venture Deals* by Brad Feld and Jason Mendelson

- *Go For No!* by Richard Fenton and Andrea Waltz

- *Man's Search for Meaning* by Viktor E. Frankl

- *Making the First Circle Work* by Randy Gage

- *The Presentation Secrets of Steve Jobs* by Carmine Gallo

- *Heartache and Hope in Haiti* by Len and Cherylann Gengel

- *The E-Myth Revisited* by Michael E. Gerber

- *Stumbling on Happiness* by Daniel Gilbert

- *Purple Cow* by Seth Godin

- *The Tipping Point* by Malcolm Gladwell

- *MOJO: How to Get it, Keep It, How to Get it Back if You Lose it* by Marshall Goldsmith

- *The Energy Bus* by Jon Gordon

- *The No Complaining Rule* by Jon Gordon

- *The Compound Effect* by Darren Hardy

- *Switch: How to Change Things When Change Is Hard* by Chip Heath and Dan Heath

- *What to Say When You Talk to Your Self* by Shad Helmstetter

- *Think and Grow Rich* by Napoleon Hill

- *Unbroken* by Laura Hillenbrand

- *The Ultimate Sales Machine* by Chet Holmes

- *Delivering Happiness* by Tony Hsieh

- *On Becoming Fearless* by Arianna Huffington

- *Who Moved My Cheese* by Spencer Johnson

- *Enchanted* by Guy Kawasaki

- *The Dream Manager* by Matthew Kelly

- *Off Balance* by Matthew Kelly

- *Profiles in Courage* by John F. Kennedy

- *Strength to Love* by Martin Luther King Jr.

- *Who Can You Trust With Your Money* by Bonnie Kirchner

- *The Art of Happiness* by the Dalai Lama

- *Transformational Speaking* by Gail Larsen

- *Three Feet from Gold* by Sharon L. Lechter and Greg S. Reid

- *How We Decide* by Jonah Lehrer

- *Getting Naked* by Patrick Lencioni

- *The Five Dysfunctions of a Team* by Patrick Lencioni

- *Selling for Fun and Profit* by Hugh Liddle

- *Fish! A Proven Way to Boost Morale and Improve Results* by Stephen C. Lundin, Harry Paul, and John Christensen

- *The Mackay MBA of Selling in the Real World* by Harvey Mackay

- *The Seven Levels of Communication* by Michael J. Maher

- *Grow Regardless* by Joe Mechlinski

- *Off-The-Wall Marketing Ideas* by Nancy Michaels and Debbi J. Karpowicz

- *QBQ! The Question Behind the Question* by John G. Miller

- *The 29% Solution* by Ivan Misner

- *Blast Off!* by Allison Maslan

- *Success is NOT an Accident* by Tommy Newberry

- *The Slight Edge* by Jeff Olson

- *Your Best Life Now* by Joel Osteen

- *Crucial Conversations* by Kerry Patterson, Joseph Grenny, Ron McMillan, and Al Switzler

- *The Brand You 50: Fifty Ways to Transform Yourself from an 'Employee' into a Brand that Shouts Distinction, Commitment, and Passion* by Tom Peters

- *Drive* by Daniel H. Pink

- *The Experience Economy* by B. Joseph Pine II and James H. Gilmore

- *The 22 Immutable Laws of Marketing* by Al Ries and Jack Trout

- *Self-Worth to Net Worth* by Cia Ricco and Belinda Rosenblum

- *The Stiletto Network* by Pamela Ryckman

- *Lean In* by Sheryl Sandberg

- *The Snowball: Warren Buffett and the Business of Life* by Alice Schroeder

- *Small Message, Big Impact* by Terri L Sjodin

- *My Beloved World* by Sonia Sotomayor

- *Surviving Your Serengeti* by Stefan Swanepoel

- *The Power of Self Confidence* by Brian Tracy

- *The Trump Card* by Ivanka Trump

- *Crush It!: Why NOW is the Time to Cash In on Your Passion* by Gary Vaynerchuk

- *The Thank You Economy* by Gary Vaynerchuk

- *Enough Already!* by Peter Walsh

- *Game Plan Selling* by Marc Wayshak

- *A Second Chance at Success* by Rob White

- *How to Be Like Walt* by Pat Williams

- *Viral Social Networking* by Stephen Woessner

- *Search Engine Optimization* by Stephen Woessner

- *Appreciation Marketing: How to Achieve Greatness through Gratitude* by Tommy Wyatt and Curtis Lewsey

One of the greatest gifts you could ask for is sitting within REACH! of you right now. It's your local library. You don't even need a dollar to your name to visit one and pick up a book that could forever change your REACH!.

REACH! Challenge

1. Review your REACH! goals that you listed at the end of Chapter 2. Go online or to your local library and find at least one book that could help you accomplish each of these goals.

2. REACH! out to your networks and ask what books they recommend.

3. Tomorrow read ten pages of a book that will influence your REACH!. When you wake up the next day, read another ten. Repeat the day after, and the next, and the next... Reading just ten pages a day will forever expand your REACH!.

Visit www.REACHTools.net for free downloadable REACH! resources.

Chapter 15

Legacy

"We are a continuum. Just as we reach back to our ancestors for our fundamental values, so we, as guardians of that legacy, must reach ahead to our children and their children. And we do so with a sense of sacredness in that reaching." – Paul Tsongas

How has the world forever changed because of you? What lasting impressions will you leave after you're gone? For many, REACH! is something that will outlive them. Even upon their very last breath on this earth, their REACH! will continue to live and perhaps even grow. Think of all the people who are no longer alive, and yet still REACH! you today.

Immediate relatives who have passed on often REACH! us regularly when we contemplate what they would have said or done. Some create legacies that impact entire nations and REACH! for generations to come. Martin Luther King Jr., Abraham Lincoln, and Mother

Teresa, are just a few examples of those who have created widespread, indefinite REACH!.

Why would anyone care about REACH!ing beyond their own life? For one, it is the only possible way to outlive your death in a way. Someday your life will end. That doesn't mean that your mission, your life's work, must end too. It can carry on forever, if you set the ball rolling now. Second, REACH!ing beyond your own life is how you can have meaningful impact on the lives of those you care about. You can create REACH! today that will influence your children and their future generations even after you are gone.

How do you create a timeless legacy or movement that outlives you? You are about to find out.

1. **Teach.**

As the saying goes: "Give a man a fish, feed him for a day. Teach a man to fish and feed him for a lifetime." Humanity was designed to perpetuate REACH!. We are designed to reproduce offspring that will carry our genes into future generations. As well, each human was created with a brain capable of both storing information and lessons from the past and using it to create a better future. One simple way to create a legacy that will outlive you is to teach others something that will positively change their lives and enable them to do the same for someone else.

Begin creating your legacy today by teaching others. Start with your children by offering them your expertise, experience, and life lessons. Volunteer your time to share your specific life skills with others who may benefit. Mentor and coach others with advice they can use to achieve their dreams. REACH! is about passing on your greatest asset, your mind, to others who may benefit from it moving forward.

2. **Lead.**

Leaders create movements by living or working in such a manner that others see the benefit in living or working that way too. Martin Luther King Jr. created a revolution through his own peaceful resistance to the status quo. He taught others the ability to fight racial inequality through non-violence and the art of standing up for any strongly held belief through peaceful protest. Great leaders are people who inspire others to grow into smarter, stronger people than they are today. Stand for something, while showing others that they can too. Work for what you want in life, and show others that they, too, have the choice to work for what they want. Your REACH! expands far and wide when you set an example for others.

3. **Change.**

When you change anything in this world, you create a legacy that may outlive you. If you build a home on a tract of land, you have created a home that will provide shelter and memories for generations to come. If you build a business, you will forever alter the trajectory of the lives of those who work for you, and perhaps the lives of those who use your goods or services. The consequences of the jobs you provide will alter the wealth of your employees, the types of homes they buy, the clothes they wear, and the size of the families they have. The job you provide may offer them the ability to get proper medical coverage, enabling them to live a longer life. The effects of offering someone a job, are so far reaching, it is almost unfathomable because not only do you directly affect the lives of those you hire, but you also change the trajectory of the lives of their children, grandchildren, and so on.

Any change you bring to the world can potentially have a "Butterfly Effect," which was coined by mathematician, meteorologist, and a pioneer of chaos theory, Edward Lorenz is the idea that a butterfly's wings might create a tiny change in the atmosphere that ultimately could create, alter, or prevent a tornado in another part of the world. Note that the butterfly does not power or directly create the tornado. The flap of its wings is simply the start of a much larger chain reaction. You have the power to create a legacy of REACH! by being that force that starts a chain reaction in someone or something that is currently stagnant, or by changing the speed and direction of someone or something that is already in motion. The changes you create have ripple effects, REACH!ing not only your intended target but potentially everyone in their networks as well.

4. **Plant.**

Planting is about changing and nourishing the landscape around you. When you plant a tree, you change the world. You change the landscape, give shade and nourishment to bugs and other creatures, and help provide oxygen for all animals to breath. According to the Arbor Day Foundation, "a mature leafy tree produces as much oxygen in a season as ten people inhale in a year" and "a single mature tree can absorb carbon dioxide at a rate of forty-eight pounds per year and release enough oxygen back into the atmosphere to support two human beings." You want to create REACH! beyond your own lifetime? When you plant seeds, you literally offer sustenance to others—and when you sustain life, you REACH!. Plant!

5. **Give.**

My final advice for creating REACH! is to be giving. Give your time, your knowledge, and your money (when you can) to those who need it most. When you give to others with no expectation of receiving anything in return, you create REACH! beyond your own mind, heart, and soul; you've given someone else seeds to plant so that they may increase their own harvest in the years to come.

In 2013, I attended the funeral of David Rubenstein, a 58-year-old husband and father of two who died following an eight-year bout with scleroderma. I had never met David, except through Facebook. His wife Robbi had long been a friend and colleague in the real estate business. And later, their son Jayme became my exceptional editor, taking this book from illegible to intelligible. I was disappointed that I never had the chance to meet David; his Facebook posts suggested that he was just the kind of guy I would have enjoyed knowing.

Then unexpectedly, at his funeral of all places, I *did* get to meet David. He spoke to me—and all mourners present that day— through his self-written eulogy, delivered by his son. No longer alive, he left his thoughts to linger in each of us, instructions to follow and even impart to others outside his network—or to disregard if we chose. I got to meet David that day, and now you will too as he makes my final point in this book: REACH! is about stretching way beyond what you perceive to be possible—past your fingertips, further than your highest dreams, and beyond death itself:

My Eulogy

By: David Rubenstein
March 11, 2013 | Temple B'Nai Shalom, Westborough, MA
As read by his son, Jayme

Because of your presence today, you either know me or you know someone who does. For my purpose, you are all the same, and I'm glad you're here. You are most welcome.

There is so much that I still want to accomplish, and now I have to ask all of you to help me... although there are still outcomes that I will affect, the hands-on stuff must be delegated. It is my expectation that, since you are here, right now, I still have influence in your life. I wrote these words... I am projecting my thoughts... and you will respond. Now, you may not respond in a manner that I am hoping for—you are still making choices in response to my suggestions.

Before I begin, there are several assumptions:

- Let us understand that I will not be looking over anyone's shoulders. I'm dead. If there is to be another "being" that I may experience; I will be attending to instances that are beyond any of your conscience understanding. I will not be here, even if I could.

- If, as I outline my thoughts for you now, you feel as though you can communicate with my soul, intentions, or any other spiritual identity; know that you are conjuring memories and subjective observations of our joined past... and that that is my intention. I want that you remember me as only you can do so. You are the only One who can and does know me in the way that You do. Within the assemblage that is here today, I exist in a finite number of instances, limited by your memories and experiences of me. As I write this, I wonder how many of your images of me would I be able to recognize.

- Some, maybe all, of you will have disturbing experiences from this exercise. This is good, too. I am now locked in to my memories of you; but you have an opportunity to redress them / or not. Just accept your ability to choose.

- Please understand that all my statements, from this point

onward, are my suggestions. Follow, as you may… and have a good life.

OK now, let's huddle-up…

Look around the space that you have gathered within. Take note of the persons who have joined this assemblage.

1. I chose to donate my physical remains to the University of Massachusetts Medical School, Anatomical Gift Program. Much of the medical guidance and treatment I received had been provided by the skillfully talented and caring staffs of UMASS Memorial and University Hospitals. This gifting was not just a way of saying "Thank you," but more importantly, for me, was to make a tangible step forward in the education of someone… anyone! It is my last definitive opportunity to do so, on this earth, and I am grateful for the chance.

2. When I selected the organizations for suggested donations, in my name, I had specific ideas for the four I chose:

a. The Baypath Humane Society was the place, from which our family adopted three great friends—Buster, Sam, and Izzy. It is, I feel, a massively humane service the people of this group perform, every day.

b. The National Eating Disorders Association became a part of our lives in 2004, when Emily became aware of her own eating disorders and decided to "be the change she wanted to see in the world." Since then, she has researched, learned, and fine-tuned a variety of skills—personal and professional—to Be That Change.

c. The Juvenile Diabetes Research Foundation came to be a part of our lives when Jayme was diagnosed with type 1 diabetes in 2005. Jayme, like his sister, took a leadership role to affect change. Using the many tools in his "toolbox," he has initiated and contributed his time and money to raise more money for type 1 research.

d. The Well Spouse Association entered our lives in 2007 when Robbi needed a friend. She was being called upon to be a single parent of young adult children during their highly stressful time of need. Their medical and financial needs were rising, the weight of our own financial burden was reaching a critical mass, and my medical situation was worsening at an accelerated pace. Robbi has friends… we both do. She is loved by a strong community of friends… But no one could know what she needed, when she was left alone to deal with all of the above, in her oneness.

Then Robbi found WSA. With them, she didn't need to vent, to listen, and to talk. All she needed to do was to Be herself. The WSA community has a mantra: "When One Is Sick, Two Need Help." The organics of this group melded with who Robbi is.

Then it happened. Being Robbi means that she must also Be The Change. She found that her own healing and health was dependent on her being a part of that for the world.

Robbi has continually benefited from, and provided

(immensely) to WSA. She started a chapter for the
Metro west area of Massachusetts.

Jayme then noted to the mourners watching intently and hanging
on his every word that that was all his father wrote.

Jayme said that when he got to the bottom of the page and realized
there was no more text, he thought to himself, "Damn. Well now
I gotta write some sort of conclusion and wrap it all up." So he sat
for a few minutes, hands poised over the keyboard, when suddenly
he felt his father say to him: "Nope... I'm good. You can all take it
from here."

What are you willing to REACH! for in order to create a legacy that
will long outlive you?

REACH! Challenge

1. List five things you are extraordinarily good at.

2. Next to each item listed, write the name of someone who would love to learn about it, how to do it, etc.

3. Over the next sixty days, commit to teaching at least one person on your list what you know. Contemplate how sharing that lesson could create a global ripple effect, REACH! beyond your own fingertips.

4. Plant something! Give the gift of oxygen to ten people a year by planting one tree every year.

5. Give. There are a million ways to give. Here are just a few. Pick one that suits your budget and your passion, then just give.

    a. Volunteer to ring a Salvation Army bell during the holidays.

    b. Clean out your closets and donate clothing to a charitable donation box.

    c. Volunteer to read books at your local nursing home.

    d. Become a Big Brother or Big Sister.

    e. Take care of pets at the local animal shelter.

    f. Volunteer to pick up litter in the community.

    g. Donate food to the local food pantry.

    h. Give money to a giving box for a charity you believe in.

Visit www.REACHTools.net for free downloadable REACH! resources.

Conclusion

"So many of our dreams at first seem impossible, then they seem improbable, and then, when we summon the will, they soon become inevitable." – **Christopher Reeve**

I'm a long retired Pop Warner cheerleader, but I still remember the first time I tried to do a full split. Boy, did it hurt. And I didn't even get all the way down on the floor. Two weeks later, it was easy. I could do a full split and bend my back leg up far enough that my head could touch my foot.

When you REACH! you stretch your all-important REACH! muscles. It only takes one small win to realize that you should REACH! for bigger goals. When you start accomplishing those bigger goals, you see the benefit of imagining huge, outrageous, seemingly impossible goals. You will accomplish those too when you REACH!. This is when life gets really, really, really good. One day you're a teenage girl sitting at a copy machine making copies; the next day you wake up and realize that the world is literally in the palm of your hand. You can be, do, and have anything you want just by wanting it. Well, it's a little more work than that but it's not hard—and it's certainly not impossible. It all comes down to one little action done repeatedly over time. It all comes down to REACH!.

Here's the last **REACH! Challenge** I have for you: Do not walk away from this book, the same person you were when you started. Be bold. Be better. Change.

Wipe out the preconceived notions of who you think you are and what you are capable of doing with your life. Up until now, your thoughts were too small. You were born to be amazing, to live your wildest dreams, and to create an army of people who want nothing more than to help get you there. You now have the knowledge and tools to REACH!. The job, the spouse, the business, the clients, the family you want… all of it is so close now. You—yah, YOU—Are you willing to dream BIG dreams? Are you willing to stretch a bit? Are you willing to get uncomfortable? Strap on your seatbelt because you are in for an amazing journey.

P.S. – In the following pages, you will find lots of ways to contact us. Please stay in touch. We want to hear all about your REACH!.

– Stacey, Ann Marie, & Christi

Resources

Visit **www.theREACHmovement.com** *for
free downloadable REACH! tools.*

*You can also REACH! out to us at:
Stacey Alcorn: stacey@theREACHmovement.com
Ann Marie DuRoss: annmarie@theREACHmovement.com
Christi Guthrie: christi@theREACHmovement.com*

Stacey   **Ann Marie**   **Christi**

A Note from Stacey

My REACH! has been accelerated these last five years due mostly to the positive inspiration of my fiancée Jay and my daughter Oshyn. They are the reasons I am brave and audacious when it comes to achieving big dreams. They root me on in everything I do. Without their support I could not be the best version of myself. Everything I do is for them.

It's really difficult to put down in writing all the people who have influenced my REACH! because REACH! has been borne out of the hundreds of thousands of people who have shaped my life thus far. My role models when it came to creating my own REACH! include my mom and dad, Sheryl and Brian. I've come to the conclusion that somehow I got to handpick the family I wanted in this life because the odds of picking a better one are one in a billion. I am who I am because of them.

As for additional REACH! role models in my life, here goes: Darren Hardy unknowingly inspired me to start this REACH! movement that continues today. Thank you for being within REACH!. As well, I am forever inspired by Len and Cherylann Gengel who are the epitome of devoted REACH!ers. As I have watched them build an orphanage in Haiti out of nothing but a last wish from their daughter Britney, they have inspired me to question over and over my own self-imposed limits. I am also inspired by my fellow board members, volunteers, employees, and home recipients of Habitat for Humanity of Greater Lowell. They have all taught me selflessness, dedication, and REACH!. Also, here's to my friends at the National Speakers Association–New England who have made me a better speaker, communicator, and teacher. I am especially grateful to Marc Wayshak, Marilee Driscoll, and Nancy Michaels, who have expanded my REACH! within the speaking industry tenfold by offering ongoing advice, sharing their contacts, and helping me refine my message.

There are some people who come along and change the course of your life forever. For me, that would be Dave Liniger. An incredible business person, a veteran, a visionary, entrepreneur, and philanthropist, Dave has never once neglected to respond to my questions or appeals for advice. Even if I had never met him, he would still be my mentor by his actions alone, but somehow I am lucky enough to call him my friend. He was the first to put me on a stage, offer me coaching, and to listen to what I had to say. And he still does.

My partners at RE/MAX and P3 Coaching & Training, Andy and Jeff, have enabled my REACH! by supporting me in my many endeavors and often challenging me to shoot higher.

How do I say thanks to Christi and Ann Marie? Well first, I should be clear that they are more than just coauthors of *REACH!*; they are also coauthors of this amazing journey I call my life. Occasionally I have been known to walk down the path of bad decisions, and they are quick to help me edit my story and help me write a better end to each of my chapters. They are extraordinary moms, and I constantly aspire to be more like them. They are the kind of girls that will get home at five o'clock to spend a few hours with their families only to go back to the office to prepare for a meeting as soon as storybooks are read and their households are happily asleep. They are the women that are baking brownies at 3 a.m. for a school bake sale because there is no other time to do it. Yes, they are women that make it look easy, but I know what it takes. They are women who quietly— and *stylishly*—endure because they know that dreaming, stretching, achieving, and networking all take determination, commitment, and drive. They make me want to be a better mom, spouse, and friend. And besides that, they are my respite from weeks and sometimes months of arduous work; I am truly rested and refueled after a night out with them.

Thank you to all the amazing people who lent their personal stories to REACH!. This book is your book as much as it is mine, Christi's, and Ann Marie's. And thank you to our editor Jayme Rubenstein who was instrumental in turning our simple manuscript into a manifesto for our REACH! movement.

I am inspired daily to write and share ideas on success. I am inspired mostly by the hundreds of amazing salespeople and employees who make up the five businesses that allow me to beat the alarm clock every morning because I cannot wait for the challenge of a new day: RE/MAX Prestige, P3 Coaching & Training, All American Title, MyLittleBlackBox.com, and Black Box Boutique. Without you all, I would have nothing to share with the world. My experiences each day are the result of you. I am humbled by and grateful for your loyalty. I am proud of your accomplishments and your dedication to your own families, and I am honored to be on the same playing field as you.

Last, but certainly not least, I wanted to write *REACH!* for me. Not the "me" that I am today, but rather the "me" I was twenty-four years ago. I wrote *REACH!* for that girl working the copy machine, that girl declined from every university she applied to with little hope of a promising future. She had no money, no network, no REACH!. I know that that "me" is out there somewhere right now with a deep-down, burning desire to do something big in life despite his or her circumstances. *REACH!* was written to implore that person to bravely look beyond his or her surroundings and see a better tomorrow. To all you "me"s out there, I am challenging you right now to dream a big dream. Then simply take one step at a time as you stretch toward that bright and amazing future. Create small wins as you achieve, and do it again, then again. Strengthen your network and lean into your advocates; you'll gain more and more of them as your momentum builds. This book was written because *you* deserve better than what today has to offer. You must be willing to REACH!.

You can find me at:
www.theREACHmovement.com
www.StaceyAlcorn.com
www.Facebook.com/StaceyAlcorn10x
and www.HuffingtonPost.com/Stacey-Alcorn

A Note from Ann Marie

I would like to thank the following people that have made this experience as coauthor of my first book possible:

To Stacey Alcorn, my business partner for too many reasons to list. First and foremost, you've allowed me the opportunity to be part of this amazing journey. You have inspired me to REACH! for things I never thought I could REACH! for. Your drive, motivation, knowledge, and insight are contagious and I thank you for that.

Thank you to Christi Guthrie for being my friend, partner in crime, motivator, and therapist since the seventh grade. The way you live life to the fullest each and every day has taught me to cherish the small things and live in the moment. Thank you for shining so brightly and continuing to be my friend and business partner.

Thanks to my parents, Ron and Carol, for truly showing me that family sticks together through thick and thin. There isn't anything they wouldn't do for their children or grandchildren. Sitting around the dinner table with an Italian meal, wine, and great conversation is all we need as long as we're together. I love you both dearly.

Thank you to my brothers, Ron and Mike, and sister-in-laws, Amy and Lisa, for being a constant support not just professionally but also for always being there to help with the kids as needed.

Thank you to my in-laws, Lucille and the late Tim DuRoss, for demonstrating how true love can get you through years of trials and tribulations, and most importantly for the son they raised whom I am lucky to call my husband.

Thank you to my husband Jeff for our two beautiful children Drew and Adriana. The three of you are the reason I am so inspired to continue REACH!ing. You have been a constant supporter and amazing father, especially when I am not there. I love you!

Finally, thanks to all of you for reading *REACH!*. I hope that we stay in touch. Make sure to continue following our REACH! journey at www.theREACHmovement.com.

A Note from Christi

The ability to REACH! and to have the opportunity for things to REACH! for requires a team of great people! I am grateful that *my* team consists of some extraordinary people. A HUGE thank you to both my parents, Bill and Beth Enwright, for living the lessons of this book and passing them onto me! They did not sit down and show me tools or techniques to achieve your dreams but rather taught by example. I thank them for not always giving me what I wanted but rather what I needed, for showing me that where you are in life is no indication of where you will end up, and for all their love and support!

I'd like to thank my husband Ryan for making me a stronger life player, for knowing and embracing my craziness, and for making me coffee every morning knowing that my work day usually starts when the kids go to bed.

Huge hugs and thanks to my kids Lily, Mack, and Michael for turning my life upside down, inside out, and sideways. They taught me the ability to juggle one hundred thoughts a second while playing hide-and-go-seek with short-term memory loss. They make me a better REACH!er, dreamer, and believer because I want to teach them by example that all things are possible!

Thanks to my sister Kelly Enwright for always following my lead when we played games together growing up. She believed me when I told her that if we colored pictures, we could sell them on our front lawn and people would buy them—and that if people didn't buy, that they would stop and watch if we performed a song and dance. Thank you for being my first best friend and still my biggest fan!

Thanks to my best friend of thirty years Danielle for understanding my brain and how I operate, for all the countless nights we laid awake dreaming of when we were older and believing that there was more than winning Miss America, and for the countless screenings of the movies Gone With The Wind and Elvis and Me to embed in my mind how Priscilla and Scarlet did not let anything come between them and their dreams!

Thanks to my family for picking up my pieces and keeping my house straight while I chase my dreams: My in-laws John and Deb Guthrie, sister- and brother-in-laws John and Amanda Daigle, and Christopher Guthrie.

Thank you to my friends: To Dave Esielionis for fueling my curiosity, referring me books, and opening my eyes and heart. Inner peace IS priceless! To Joannie Berthold for teaching me that it's not the size of the dog in the fight but the size of the fight in the dog. And to Tara Bedard for skipping alongside with me, enjoying life, and doing "all the things."

Thanks to all the people I have REACH!ed out to for kindly showing me the way, sometimes giving me the key to unlock a door, and most importantly believing in me and what I was REACH!ing for.

With confidence we gain momentum; inspired, we take the climb; and with a team behind us, we are able to stand at the top of all of our dreams!

A special thanks to my great grandmother, my nana, Elizabeth Higgison for always being my guiding light and for giving me a strong belief in things unseen and faith in things felt. God rest your soul.

And last but not least, thank you to my business partners Ann Marie Duross and Stacey Alcorn for believing in me! Specifically, thanks Ann Marie for teaching me the social skills needed for success while growing up, for always fighting me for the "Golden Ticket"—and the music! Thanks Stacey for always saying, "So?," "Who Cares?," "Ok!," and "Let's Do It!" You have opened my eyes wider; now I see it all and I am forever thankful!

Make sure to keep following our REACH!. You can find me at www. theREACHmovement.com, www.HuffingtonPost.com/Christi-Guthrie, and www.ChristiGuthrie.com. And girls, if you love a little style like I do, please check out www.MyLittleBlackBox.com. Our subscription jewelry and accessory business is where me, Ann Marie, and Stacey truly realized the power of our REACH!.